The Hamlyn Guide to
Gardening Skills

Peter Blackburne-Maze

Hamlyn
London · New York · Sydney · Toronto

Acknowledgements

Line artwork by Ron Hayward and Norman Barber.

Colour photographs by Peter Blackburne-Maze, The Harry Smith Horticultural Photographic Collection and Michael Warren.

Black and white photographs by Amateur Gardening, Bob Andrews Ltd, Black and Decker Ltd, Peter Blackburne-Maze, Robert Corbin, Country Life, John Cowley, Flymo Ltd, The Fyba Pot Company, Garotta Products Ltd, Hozelock Ltd, Imperial Chemical Industries Ltd, Patrick Johns, Pan Britannica Industries Ltd, May and Baker Ltd, Murphy Chemical Ltd, PaiceSetter Ltd, Sinclair Horticulture and Leisure plc, The Harry Smith Horticultural Photographic Collection and Wilson Grimes Products.

In addition,
the author would like to thank East Malling Research Station and R. Harkness and Co. Ltd for their help and co-operation.

The publishers would like to thank Mrs I. D. Sinfield for allowing them use of her garden for photographic purposes on the cover of this book.

First published 1985 by
The Hamlyn Publishing Group Limited
London . New York . Sydney . Toronto
Astronaut House, Feltham, Middlesex, England

ISBN 0 600 30545 7

Phototypeset in England by
Wyvern Typesetting Limited, Bristol
on Linotron 202 in 11 on 12 pt Palatino

Printed in Yugoslavia

Contents

Introduction

Gardening as we think of it today started in the Middle East and China about four thousand years ago and has probably been carried out in Europe for about half that time. It no longer requires the vast resources it once did and nowadays anyone with a patch of land, no matter how small, can turn it into a garden. Even people living in blocks of flats can garden now; maybe not on the same scale but growing-bags, window boxes, hanging baskets and all manner of containers make it possible to cultivate plants anywhere. That, though, is another story; it is with 'garden gardening' that we are concerned here.

Although a large proportion of the population have gardens many of these are neglected simply because the householders have neither the time nor the inclination to look after them. There are, however, an increasing number of first-time gardeners who are full of enthusiasm and whose lack of knowledge is the only limiting factor. These are the people at whom this book is primarily aimed and a glance at the contents page will show that the subject begins with the one feature that is common to all gardens: the soil.

Science can play an important part in gardening, but no beginner should think that they need a degree in botany or chemistry to succeed. It does help, though, to have a down-to-earth understanding (if that is the right expression) of how a plant works and what is going on in the soil.

Over the years, and in spite of the advances made in chemicals, plant breeding and labour-saving devices, surprisingly few of the basic principles of gardening have changed to any extent. Digging, for example, is still fundamental and so are the implements used to carry it out. Once these basic principles have been mastered, a whole new world is opened up and the newcomer can join in on equal terms with the expert. Gardening is as easy as falling off a log; after all, plants will grow whether we look after them or not. All we are doing is helping Nature and sometimes bending her in a direction that suits us. The art of gardening is knowing just how far Nature can be bent; and in which direction.

The Soil

The first thing that any would-be gardener must realize is that soil is a desperately complicated material, teeming with life and with biological and chemical changes going on the whole time. The interaction of all the inhabitants and processes is still not fully understood but enough is known to convince us that soil really is something rather special and that if it is abused, problems will arise that can seriously affect our gardening. Soil is made up of many things but they can all be classified as being either solid, liquid or gas.

Composition

The main solid material is ground-up rock and minerals and it is the size and proportion of the individual particles that determine the soil type. Clay and silt have a high percentage of very small particles, loam is fairly evenly divided between large, medium and small and sandy

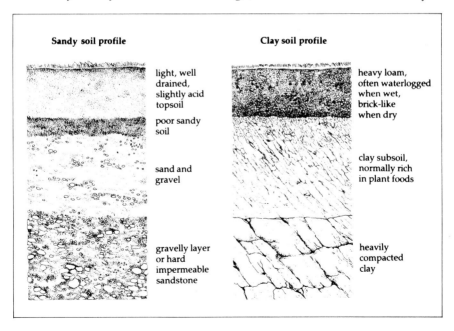

Sandy soil profile

light, well drained, slightly acid topsoil

poor sandy soil

sand and gravel

gravelly layer or hard impermeable sandstone

Clay soil profile

heavy loam, often waterlogged when wet, brick-like when dry

clay subsoil, normally rich in plant foods

heavily compacted clay

soils consist principally of large grains. This is where the word 'texture' comes in. A soil is said to have a fine texture when it contains a great many very small particles, as in clay and silt. Sandy soil, on the other hand, has a coarse texture whilst loam is medium textured.

These particles, however, are not simply a mass of individual bits, each totally independent of all others; they are held together in varying sized blocks, or crumbs. This is best explained by thinking of each particle as a single marble. If you have a large box of marbles, they can all move around at will; you will find a situation like this in a desert or on a sandy beach where there is no cohesion between the grains of sand. If, though, the marbles are put into a number of polythene bags before going into the box, a completely different situation exists and one far more akin to garden soil. The particles are bonded together and it is this that gives a soil its 'structure'.

The maintenance of a good soil structure is vital. Even more than the texture, it is the structure that governs the ease with which air can reach the roots, surplus water can drain away and the roots themselves can penetrate to their full extent. All of which combines to give strong and healthy plants.

Another solid material, and in many respects the most important, is organic matter. This is the decomposed, or partially decomposed, remains of anything that was once alive and we will be dealing with it fully in the section on fertilizers and feeding plants. The third thing that can be thought of as solid covers all the millions of living organisms present in the soil. These can vary in size from earthworms right down to single-celled bacteria.

Hardly surprisingly, the liquid content of the soil is made up largely of water. Clearly, this is essential for plant growth but it has two other very important jobs. The first is that most of the soil's living inhabitants are dependent on water; without it, they become inactive and unable to carry out the vital work of breaking down organic matter and liberating the plant foods stored in it. The other role played by water is that of dissolving and transporting minerals in a form that can be absorbed by the roots.

When we come to talk about gases in the soil, the two we are most concerned with are oxygen and carbon dioxide. As all parts of a plant, both above and below ground, need oxygen to survive and operate properly, it is vital that the soil is sufficiently open to allow air to penetrate to the roots. It is equally important that the carbon dioxide given off by the roots is able to escape. A badly compacted soil will prevent this exchange taking place and the plants will inevitably suffer.

An even more basic reason for having air spaces in a soil is that it is through them that surplus water drains away. If they do not exist, the water remains in the soil and the whole thing becomes waterlogged; once again, to the detriment of the plants.

Soil types

Having had a brief look at the soil, we can now understand better why different types have different characteristics.

Soils can be broadly described as heavy, medium or light.

Heavy soils   Clay and silt are characterized by their fine texture and, until they have been under cultivation for some years, their poor structure. Their fineness means that they are frequently poorly drained and this can lead to a considerable time being taken to dry out and warm up in the spring. In a dry summer, they tend to become rock hard. On the positive side, heavy soils are the last to feel the effects of drought and, potentially, they are the most fertile of all because they retain plant foods for a considerable time.

Medium soil or loam   This is rather a loose term as it is more of a description than a type of soil. However, the generally accepted definition is that it is medium textured, well supplied with organic matter and has a good and stable structure. It is the kind of soil that all gardeners would like but few are lucky enough to have.

Light soils   These are normally very sandy and coarse textured and this leads to a loose structure until there is enough organic matter in the ground to stabilize and improve it. Plant foods are easily washed out (leached) by the rain so they are usually starved and the rain itself quickly drains away. However, light soils are easy to cultivate and they warm up early in the spring. Plants get established in them quickly but need sustaining if they are to give of their best. Being sandy, light soils are nearly always acidic and usually need regular applications of lime to correct this so that plants are better able to make use of the available nutrients.

Special soils   We now come to what might be called 'special' soils and the first is those which overlie chalk or limestone. Their main feature is that they are normally strongly alkaline and, as we shall see, not all plants will tolerate this as some of the essential elements are rendered unavailable to the plants. Apart from this, they tend to behave in a similar way to other soils with the same texture, for you can find heavy, medium or light soils on top of chalk.

Peat soils, on the other hand, are far less common. They are extremely rich in organic matter and, whilst this might seem ideal, you can have too much of a good thing. They tend to be light and acidic and can often be improved by adding a proportion of heavier soil. This makes them less prone to drying out and enables them to retain plant foods better.

Acid or alkaline?
The question of whether a soil is acidic or alkaline may seem of academic interest to a beginner but it has an important bearing on the types of plant that will flourish in it. For example, all plants will grow in a slightly acid soil but, as the chalk/lime content increases, things like rhododendrons, azaleas and most of the heathers will begin to show signs of distress and eventually die. Exactly the same happens at the opposite end of the scale as the acidity increases.

We can measure the acidity or alkalinity of a soil quite easily nowadays and the answer is expressed in terms of its pH value. Although a pH of 7 is considered neutral (neither acid nor alkaline) for scientific purposes, in gardening terms pH 6.5 to 7 is neutral. A figure higher than this indicates alkalinity and one lower, acidity. Naturally, the degree increases the further the number gets away from neutral. The majority of soils fall into the range pH 5 to 8.

Although the best pH for different plants varies, 6 to 6.5 is a good range to aim for as this is certainly the best for vegetables; it is, though, far from critical. Raising or lowering the pH of a soil by a couple of units or so is quite easy. To raise it by one pH unit (whole number) to make the soil less acid, apply about 500 g per m²(1 lb per sq yd) of ground chalk or limestone. Acidifying the soil is most easily done by working in plenty of peat, and this also improves the physical structure. Powdered sulphur or iron sulphate applied at a rate of 120 g per m² (4 oz per sq yd) is also effective but much more expensive.

Having already mentioned that the pH of a soil will affect their availability, this seems an appropriate point at which to have a quick look at the more important nutrient elements.

Altogether, some twelve elements are essential to plants and all are found in varying amounts in the soil. From the gardening point of view, they are divided into either major elements or trace elements; not in respect of their importance but of the quantities in which they are required by the plants. Trace elements are sometimes called 'minor' elements but this is confusing as it could imply that they are not so important. All are essential.

The three elements in most need of regular replenishing are nitrogen (N), phosphorus (P) and potassium or potash (K) and the whole subject will be covered in much more detail in the chapter on Feeding Plants (see page 18).

Although kits for determining the various nutrient levels in the soil can be very useful on occasions, one's own eyes are more reliable in the first instance. In other words, if plants are growing satisfactorily, testing the soil is usually unnecessary.

It is more important to find out whether the soil is acid or alkaline, and to what degree (the pH). This can be measured using either a chemical kit, similar to the nutrient one, or a pH meter like the one illustrated. A knowledge of the soil pH will give a good idea of which sorts of plants will flourish and which will probably fail.

If it has been established that a soil requires lime, the best time to apply it is after autumn/winter digging so that the winter rains wash it well in. By the way, never apply lime or chalk straight on top of farmyard manure as ammonia gas will be given off and much of the nitrogen content of the manure will be lost.

Soil Cultivations

Let's start off with one of the golden rules of gardening. The soil should only be worked when it is in a fit state. If it is too wet, the structure can easily be ruined and may take weeks to restore. On the other hand, if it is too dry, a sandy soil is likely to lose a lot of moisture and clay will be so hard that cultivations will be impossible. Aim at a happy medium. Now to the actual cultivations.

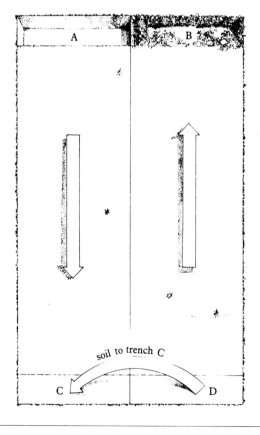

When digging a reasonably large plot, it is a help to divide it in two and tackle one half at a time as follows. Dig out a trench at A and pile the soil at B. The next strip of soil is turned over and forward into trench A. Continue back down the plot until you are left with trench C. Fill this with the soil from D and carry on digging until you get to the final trench. This is filled with soil B. If the plot is not being dug in two halves, the soil from A is simply put at the far end and used to fill trench D

Digging
Just as the farmer's basic method of tilling the soil is ploughing, the gardener's is digging. This is normally carried out when land is being worked for the first time or when a crop has just been cleared from ground already under cultivation. A spade is the usual tool but, on heavy land, the job is often easier with a fork; the choice depends on whether or not the soil will hold together when lifted.

There are several reasons for digging, the most important being to aerate the soil and to create a tilth so that seeds can be sown and seedlings planted. Digging will bury any weeds and plant debris and is an excellent way of incorporating bulky organic matter into the soil. The right way to dig is to hold the spade or fork as near vertical as you can and drive it in to its full depth so that the soil is moved as deeply as possible. This also ensures that anything you want buried really is well covered.

Digging to one spade's depth is called 'single digging'. In a brand new garden, or one that has been neglected for a number of years, a more effective way of bringing the ground into working order is 'double digging'. Whilst the principle is the same, the difference is that the bottom of each trench is thoroughly loosened to a full fork's depth. This doubles the depth to which roots can easily penetrate, thereby greatly improving the quality of the plants. Vegetables may be expected to yield up to 30 per cent more as a result of double digging and, in the case of broad beans, the crop can be very nearly doubled. Although new and neglected gardens benefit most from double digging, it should be done on established plots every four years or so to break up the compacted underground layer of soil that develops as a result of continual single digging.

Creating a tilth
Once land has been dug, leave it rough until shortly before you want to sow or plant. It is then broken down and levelled by using either a hand cultivator or by working it down with the back of a fork. This will normally be enough for planting, but for sowing, it will need to be raked to create a finer tilth and to remove any stones.

Hoeing   Once a crop is established, be it flowers or vegetables, weeds are sure to appear before long and should be killed as soon as possible. A hoe is the usual tool for doing this but, during prolonged wet spells, a weedkiller such as Weedol will deal with them safely and leave the soil uncontaminated.

There are two types of hoe: the swan-neck (or draw hoe) and the Dutch hoe. The difference is that you work forwards with the

When soil is in this condition, it should be left alone until it has dried out. Even walking on it can turn it into mud which will ruin the structure for many months.

Although this might appear to be too much of a good thing, stout footwear is essential when digging. Not only will you do the job better but you are unlikely to get blisters; in any case, the heavy wear and tear will ruin flimsy shoes in no time at all.

When any large plot is being dug for the first time, it is better to divide it in two before starting and to take each half separately; the diagram on page 12 shows the reason for this. The digging should be done in the late autumn or winter and the soil is then left in a rough state in order to expose the greatest area to the breaking-down action of the winter weather.

A method of digging called 'ridging' is not often seen these days but it exposes an even greater surface area to the weather than ordinary digging. This can be particularly beneficial where the ground is heavy or is being dug for the first time. Each line of digging is about 1 m (3 ft) wide and the soil is placed in a ridge down the centre rather than spread level.

This is one of the most useful types of hand cultivator. It can be used for breaking down dug soil in readiness for sowing or planting, or for working the land between rows of standing crops – either to remove a surface crust after heavy rain or for incorporating fertilizer.

A draw hoe with a difference and a type that is particularly good for weeding. The thin blade slips neatly beneath the weeds without disturbing the roots of neighbouring plants. Always keep the blade sharp.

A Swoe being used amongst shrubs to keep weeds down. The great advantage of this sort over the draw hoe is that it can be worked very easily right up to and around the stems of the plants.

Mechanical cultivators are very useful for creating a fine and deep tilth but should never be thought of as a substitute for digging; nor should they be used when the ground is wet or they will simply smear the soil and get clogged up.

swan-neck and backwards with the Dutch. For those who cannot make up their mind which is best, there is a very useful tool called a Swoe, which can be worked either way.

Stick to the basics

These are the main cultivations and all are carried out quite easily with the tools mentioned. There are, of course, many other implements available; some are very useful but others, quite honestly, are best left well alone as they often cost a lot of money and are no better than cheaper and more versatile ones. As you get more experienced, you may well want a greater selection of tools but, to start off with, stick to the basics.

Whilst on the subject, mention should be made of mechanical rotavators and cultivators. These can be a boon in a large garden but are an expensive luxury in a small one, unless you hire them. Added to this, there is a definite skill in knowing when and where their use is appropriate and this will only come with experience.

With all this talk of digging and hoeing, one is inclined to forget that there are a considerable number of gardeners who advocate either minimum cultivation or none at all. For the most part, this type of gardening is based on building up successive layers of bulky organic matter for the plants to grow in. Although it can be very effective under the right circumstances, it can be a total failure if conditions are wrong or if it is not carried out properly. Anyone wishing to try it should certainly read one of the many excellent books on the subject beforehand.

Tools are expensive items and, whether or not they are stainless steel, should always be kept clean. Dirty or rusty tools not only fail to work effectively but they will soon wear out. A spade, in particular, should be kept bright or it will never slice through the soil.

A wire brush is the very thing for cleaning soil off awkward shaped tools but this should be allowed to dry first or the brush will suffer. If tools are not going to be used for some time, they should be given a final wipe over with an oily rag to stop them rusting.

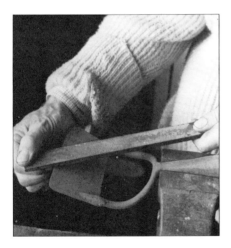

Hoes must be sharp at all times or they will simply push the weeds out complete with their roots. They can then easily root again in damp weather whereas those that have been cleanly cut off are sure to die.

When fixing a new handle, shape the end so that it fits really tightly into the socket on the tool and always secure it with a nail or small screw to prevent it wobbling about.

Feeding Plants

We must now turn our attention to the 'inner plant'. What are we going to feed it on? Fortunately, a plant's needs are modest compared with our own but there are still those twelve elements that are absolutely essential for healthy growth. These, as already mentioned, are divided into major elements – nitrogen, phosphorus, potassium, calcium, magnesium and sulphur, and trace elements – iron, boron, manganese, zinc, copper and molybdenum.

In Nature, plants get these elements mainly from decayed vegetation and bird and animal droppings. In the garden, it is not quite as simple as that because we remove the plants after they have died and there is a definite shortage of animals. This means that we have to supply most of the food ourselves.

Garden compost
This provides a partial answer. Not only does it supply the soil with many of the elements that plants require, albeit in small quantities, but it adds vital organic matter to it as well. In addition, it enables us to make excellent use of all the plant debris that would otherwise have to be got rid of by some other means. By the way, the type of compost we are talking about here, garden compost, has no connection at all with the seed and potting composts we buy in bags and use for raising and growing plants.

As far as returning plant nutrients to the ground is concerned, garden compost should never be regarded as a major source because only a very small percentage of what is taken out is returned in this way. Although the remains of most flowers can find their way back into the soil in the form of compost, a much greater proportion of the plants we grow is eaten and lost. Because of this, compost should always be used in conjunction with fertilizers. Nevertheless, compost does make a contribution, particularly with the trace elements. Its most important benefit, though, lies in adding bulky organic matter to the soil and, to understand this, we have to go back to fundamentals.

Bulky organic matter

The nature of a soil is determined by its 'parent material', that is, the underlying rock or other substance, such as clay, from which it is formed. In order to make soil, the parent material first has to be broken down by the weather, and other natural forces, into small particles that will enable seeds to germinate and take root.

Once this occurs, plants will grow and their dead remains will be taken back into the soil to be decomposed. At this point, a cycle begins. The dead vegetation is broken down by naturally occurring bacteria, fungi and other soil organisms but, in order to survive, these need dead vegetation to feed on; hence the cycle. The non-existence or removal of one or other of these elements will break the chain.

The practical implications of all this in the garden are that a soil is only fertile and able to support the high standard of plant life that we expect if it is well supplied with organic matter and its accompanying micro-organisms. Another part that bulky organic matter has to play, and this applies to rotted farmyard manure as well as garden compost, is the direct physical effect it has on the soil. This will occur in all soils though it is, hardly surprisingly, the worst soils that benefit most.

For those who are able to get it, farmyard manure is magnificent stuff but, like garden waste, it must also be composted before it is used. Raw manure contains a lot of straw and this must be well rotted before it is dug in or there is a chance that it will rob the ground of nitrogen when it starts to decompose. In spite of the almost mystical properties attributed to manure, its nutrient content, in fact, is very similar to that of garden compost. After all, both are decomposed vegetation.

Peat and pulverized bark are two other sources of bulky organic matter and these have the advantage of being clean, pleasant to use, completely free of weed seeds and other 'nasties' and readily available from garden centres. They are, though, apt to be quite expensive if large quantities are needed. Neither has any nutrient value and their use, for most of us, is really confined to the preparation of seed beds, mulching and for mixing into sowing and potting composts. Peat is a very good material for acidifying chalky soil if you want to grow lime-hating plants.

Well-rotted bulky organic matter has truly remarkable properties. At one and the same time, it is capable of holding a large amount of moisture whilst still being full of air and it is because of these opposite abilities that it is able to open up and aerate clay soils and yet help sandy ones to retain far more water and plant nutrients.

Emphasis throughout has been placed on *bulky* organic matter because it is its very bulk that has the physical effect on the soil.

Organic fertilizers like hoof and horn will improve the soil chemically and biologically but they will do nothing to benefit its structure in the short term; they are applied at far too low a rate to have any effect at all.

The compost heap

When making garden compost, anything of vegetative origin can go into the compost heap, the main thing being a good mixture of soft and not so soft material.

If you have a small garden and not much raw material, probably the most convenient way of composting is to buy a bin specially made for the job. On the other hand, with a large garden and plenty of waste vegetation, the traditional type of heap is likely to be better. In either case, you make the compost in exactly the same way.

The heap or bin is filled up with layers of raw material and, at every 15 to 23 cm (6 to 9 in) of depth, an activator is sprinkled on before the next layer is introduced.

If the heap cannot be completed in one go, either the lid should be put back on the bin after each filling or the heap should be covered to keep the heat in and the rain out. This heat is produced by the micro-organisms during the decomposition process and the generation of a high temperature 49 to 60°C (120 to 140°F) shows that the heap really is 'working' well. Compost will be formed without it but not nearly so quickly.

This is where the activator comes in. In essence, it is a material containing a high proportion of nitrogen for the micro-organisms to feed on. One is sometimes advised to use sulphate of ammonia instead of a proprietary brand in the mistaken belief that it is cheaper and just as good. It is neither. It may be a little cheaper per kilogram but, on its own, it is definitely not a good thing to add to a compost heap because it creates conditions far too acid for the micro-organisms to thrive in. This involves further expense on something like lime to neutralize the heap. All part of the myth that proprietary products cost more.

The major elements

It is time now to have a quick look at the parts played by the more important elements as this can help in understanding why they are needed.

Nitrogen is the one most in demand; its main contribution is growth and the production of new leaves. It also gives bulk and size to a plant and that rich green colour which we associate with health.

Phosphorus (phosphates) encourages root development and the quick establishment of young plants as well as hastening maturity in

Provided the type of raw material is right and there is sufficient air and moisture available, the size and shape of a compost heap depends largely on your own circumstances.

The main use for garden compost is to add bulky organic matter to the soil. Where the subsoil has become compacted or has never been cultivated, double digging and the incorporation of compost will double the depth to which roots can penetrate.

When garden compost is going to be dug in, it should be barrowed onto the plot and spread evenly before starting to dig; this will show you whether there is enough or not. When digging it in, it should never just be put in the bottom of the trench and then covered, but spread over the face of the trench as well so that the full depth of soil benefits.

For small gardens, or where the amount of raw material is limited, purpose-made containers are the answer. They have a capacity of about 2 m³ (70 cu ft), keep everything neat and tidy and are virtually indestructible. The best idea is to have two bins or heaps of compost, one being built and one ready to use.

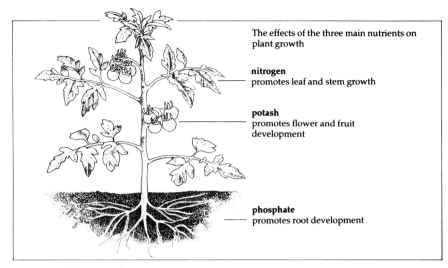

The effects of the three main nutrients on plant growth

nitrogen
promotes leaf and stem growth

potash
promotes flower and fruit development

phosphate
promotes root development

vegetables and fruit.

Potassium (potash) to some extent controls the effect of nitrogen by inducing sturdiness and toughness in plants which results in a more balanced growth. It improves disease resistance and gives a good colour to flowers and fruit as well as encouraging them.

Magnesium is a part of the chlorophyll molecule, the green substance that is present in most plants. Without chlorophyll, plants cannot use the energy of the sun to help them grow so the importance of magnesium is obvious.

Being able to diagnose shortages of specific elements is, perhaps, more of academic interest than practical value but the ability to recognize when a plant is not receiving all that it needs is fundamental to good gardening. For example, trouble should always be suspected if growth stops and foliage begins to turn yellow in the middle of the growing season.

Fertilizers
The way to correct a deficiency or, better still, to prevent one occurring, is to apply plant foods to the ground in the form of fertilizers. These, however, come in so many shapes and sizes that it can be bewildering to a beginner. For a start, they may be of organic or inorganic origin. They may be found in granular form, as liquids to be diluted and as crystals that have to be dissolved before use.

Organic fertilizers Those such as hoof and horn, bonemeal and dried blood, generally release their nutrients slower than inorganic ones so they tend to last longer in the soil. Against this, one has to put their normally lower nutrient value, their higher cost and the fact that many of them only supply one element.

Inorganic fertilizers These are usually quicker acting, are applied at lower rates and normally contain nitrogen, phosphates and potash. The belief that inorganic fertilizers are somehow harmful to the soil is greatly exaggerated. The application rates of fertilizers is never high enough to have any effect at all and plants certainly cannot tell one from the other. It is the failure to add bulky organic matter to the soil that can lead to problems, not the use of fertilizers.

Granular fertilizers These are most commonly used outdoors. They are applied to perennial plants, trees, shrubs and fruit every spring and to annual crops shortly before sowing or planting (a base dressing) and again halfway through their life (a top dressing).

Liquid fertilizers These are mainly used to feed plants under glass and in the home. They are quick acting but are soon used up, so have to be applied regularly when the plants are growing. Although their outdoor use is limited, they are very useful during periods of drought as they provide food and water at the same time.

Another type of fertilizer is called a 'foliar feed'. This, as the name suggests, is applied as a spray to the leaves of plants. The nutrients are absorbed by the plants extremely quickly but only in small quantities so they should never be regarded as an alternative to root feeding.

Their main function is to act as a tonic to the plant, such as when it needs that little extra to lift it from being a good specimen to an exceptional one or, more usually, when the plant is not operating at full efficiency. This can arise shortly after planting or when the roots have suffered some other form of damage.

Trace elements Another very important use for foliar feeds is in the correction of trace element deficiencies. Fortunately quite rare, these can arise for a number of reasons but are most frequently met with on chalky soils where certain elements, notably iron, manganese and boron, are unavailable to the plants because of the strong alkalinity. The long-term answer is to correct this or to apply trace elements annually in the form of a sequestrene but, as a first aid measure, a foliar feed containing at least iron and manganese, like Maxicrop or Instant Bio, is the solution.

Application Finally, a word on the application of fertilizers. In most cases you will be dealing with concentrated materials which can damage plants if not properly applied. They should always be used at the recommended rate and, particularly with granular fertilizers, they must be applied evenly and over the whole area being treated, not just around the base of plants. Where possible, these should also be watered in after application.

Apply a base-dressing just before sowing or planting when conditions are right (not too wet or bone dry). Sprinkle it evenly over the whole area.

Rake the fertilizer well in to distribute it throughout the top two centimetres or so of soil. Note that the soil surface is not being trodden on or compacted.

Foliar feeding is an excellent way of getting nutrients into a plant quickly. This can be useful if the plant is suffering in any way or simply as a shot-in-the-arm to supplement other fertilizers.

These roses are being top-dressed after the first flush of flowers is over in order to encourage further flowering. Sprinkle the fertilizer evenly over the whole border and lightly rake or hoe it in, following that by watering.

Watering and Water Conservation

It seems strange that, in a country where we perpetually moan about the bad weather, nearly every summer should bring the problem of how to keep our plants alive during seemingly inevitable water shortages.

If you think about it though, most of our rain falls at the time of year when plants need it least. What really counts is the rainfall from April to September and as this varies greatly from region to region it is clearly impossible to generalize. However, we can say that in many areas the need to water will arise in the majority of summers whilst, at the other extreme, it may be needed only one or two years in every ten, if at all.

Another certainty is that there are definite times in the annual life of a plant when any shortage of water will be harmful. Quite obviously, established trees and shrubs are the least vulnerable because of their extensive root systems. With other decorative plants though, and we can include lawns here, the need for watering is going to be more frequent.

When we consider vegetables, quite a lot is known about their water needs as, being a food crop, much research has gone into their commercial production, the results of which can be very helpful to gardeners. Here are some examples. Peas and beans need plenty of water when they are in flower and again when the pods are developing. Root crops, such as carrots and parsnips, need a steady supply throughout their life to give even growth and to prevent them splitting, something which nearly always occurs if heavy rain follows a drought.

With potatoes, a thorough soaking when the young tubers are about the size of marbles will increase the yield and often means earlier lifting. Brassicas, celery and other 'green' vegetables, such as lettuces, always give of their best when they have ample water during the two weeks before maturity whilst quick-growing crops like radishes should never be allowed to run short at all or they become woody and often 'bolt' (develop a flower head). Summer and autumn cauliflowers also come into this category; any check to their development leads to the curds bursting when still quite small.

How much?

The next point is just as important as knowing when to water as it involves the amount of water that should be applied at any one time. What so often occurs is that, once the surface of the soil has been wetted, the gardener stops watering. Except in the case of recently sown seeds, this does more harm than good.

What happens is that roots are encouraged to form in the moist upper layer of soil instead of continuing to grow downwards. Not only will these surface roots be unable to supply the plant with its needs but they will also be the first to dry out again. This is what has given rise to the wildly inaccurate notion that, once you start watering, you have to carry on, come rain or shine. Nothing could be further from the truth; if the ground is given a good soaking at the right time, this will usually be enough to last for a week or more, even during a severe drought.

When you water, therefore, give at least 1.5 cm ($\frac{1}{2}$ in) at a time and, preferably, 2.5 cm (1 in). If using a sprinkler, this is easily worked out by putting empty tins or jam jars over the area being watered and measuring how much collects in them. To give an idea of the sort of quantities we are talking about, 1050 litres (230 gals) are needed to supply 2.5 cm (1 in) over 42 m^2 (50 sq yd) whilst, for a medium loam soil, 18 litres per m^2 (4 gal per sq yd) are required for it to penetrate to 30 cm (1 ft) deep; far more than most people would think.

Sources of water

As regards the different sources from which water may be obtained, the obvious one is a tap and, if you have not already got one outside, it is certainly worth installing; struggling to fit a hose to the kitchen tap can be very unpopular and messy. The most convenient size is a 1-cm ($\frac{1}{2}$-in) one with a thread on it for attaching the hose. Outside taps must have a stopcock indoors so that they can be turned off and drained for the winter to prevent frost damage.

Some people feel that tapwater is not particularly good for plants and they certainly seem to do better after a downpour. However, the only instance where it is likely to be harmful is when lime-hating plants are watered with hard water as the lime content can upset them.

Rainwater is bound to be best as it is normally neutral (and natural) with no chemicals deliberately added. It does need to be stored and, for this, plastic water butts are probably better than metal as they are likely to last longer and the chance of rust contamination is avoided. They must have a lid, too, as standing water becomes full of algae if exposed to the light.

There are many other places where water can be found including ponds, wells and streams and all are perfectly satisfactory for garden use, provided they are in no way contaminated. All these are more or less orthodox sources of water but, in an emergency, one may have to turn to the unusual. Used bathwater is quite satisfactory and has saved the life of many a plant in a long, hot summer. The rinsing water from a washing machine is also usable. Neither could be called ideal but at least they are water.

Methods of application
The methods of applying water in a garden are many and varied and, whilst the traditional watering can is handy for small areas, such as seed-beds, something capable of giving a far greater quantity is needed for larger areas.

The simplest and cheapest is a hose with either a rose or a variable nozzle fitted to the end. This can simply be held or it can be tied to the handle of a fork stuck in the ground so that it plays over an area while you get on with something else. More sophisticated and, consequently, more expensive are the different types of sprinkler. These have clear advantages but you should never be tempted to buy an expensive and complicated gadget when something half the price and much simpler will do just as well. Most sprinklers are made of plastic and, although this is corrosion-free and cheaper than metal, it is not as strong. Special care should be taken to avoid cross-threading and to keep the threads free of grit and soil.

Hoses have also undergone a change. Plastic has taken over from rubber and, although cheaper, it is apt to become kinked and unmanageable when cold. The latest thing in hoses is a woven type, with or without a polythene lining, which is reeled onto a spool rather like a fireman's hose. This is very much handier, takes up virtually no room at all and, with care, should last as long as the old sort. One has to be slightly guarded about this as they have not been on the market for long enough to judge their life expectancy.

Conserving soil moisture
With all this talk about watering, one might be forgiven for thinking that it is inevitable. Frequently it is but a lot can be done to make better use of the water that already exists in the soil. First of all, there are soil cultivations. As we have seen, if roots can penetrate deeply, they are far better able to reach the cooler and moister soil that lies well below the surface.

Then there is the organic matter content of the soil. If this is kept at a high level by the regular addition of garden compost, the water-

The simplest sprinkler costs very little. It throws water out in a circular pattern which is fine for such places as a lawn with neighbouring flower beds but is less effective if the area is rectangular, such as rows of vegetables.

A much better system for the vegetable garden is to use a spray line type (shown here on a lawn for clarity). The length of the watered area depends on the length of the line and the width can be adjusted by altering the water pressure at the tap.

The oscillating sprinkler is also suitable for rectangular areas as the delivery head rocks from one side to the other. Some models can also be made to stay in one position so that the water is only delivered to a specific patch of land.

A good way of watering deep-rooted flowers and vegetables is to sink an old field drain or flower pot near them and fill this up with water as and when required.

holding capacity of a light soil will be greatly increased and on heavy land the drainage will be improved.

Another way of conserving water is to put a good thick layer of compost, peat or bark down on the ground (a mulch); this will help enormously in preventing evaporation from the soil. It must, however, be applied when the ground is moist, such as in the early spring or straight after watering, as it will have just the opposite effect on a dry soil and actually stop the penetration of water. Black polythene is just as efficient as a mulch, but, of course, it adds no organic matter to the soil (see page 30).

Incidentally, the belief that hoeing conserves water by creating a 'dust mulch' is quite wrong; it can actually harm plants by damaging the surface roots. On the plus side, hoeing is beneficial in removing weeds which would be in competition with the plants for water. Planting firmly and keeping the soil well consolidated will also help it to retain moisture. Something else we should do is keep the garden as sheltered as possible by planting hedges and windbreaks, as wind is notorious for drying out plants.

Plants sown in autumn are much less likely to suffer from drought than spring-sown ones as they will be well established by the time the danger period arrives the following summer.

It may sound strange but correct watering can actually *save* water. For example, it is normally best to water outdoor plants towards the end of the day so that they have the cool night in which to absorb moisture and evaporation will be minimal. Watering seeds and seedlings with a watering can is much more economical than using a sprinkler.

A totally different approach involves conserving water which is otherwise lost through the leaves of plants. Normally this is not too much of a problem because established plants absorb water with their roots at about the same rate that they lose it through the leaves.

However, recently planted subjects, be they cabbage seedlings or quite large shrubs, have not got a large enough root system to sustain them and are apt to suffer in warm weather.

One excellent way around this is to use a spray that will temporarily coat the leaves with a sort of plastic and thereby reduce transpiration almost to a standstill. There is an aerosol on the market called 'Spray and Save' which does this admirably and is especially effective on newly planted conifers.

So you see, although water is vitally important, there are many ways in which we can reduce the amount we have to use. Always remember though, if plants need water, be sure to give it or they will only suffer.

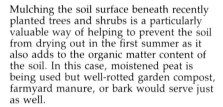

Mulching the soil surface beneath recently planted trees and shrubs is a particularly valuable way of helping to prevent the soil from drying out in the first summer as it also adds to the organic matter content of the soil. In this case, moistened peat is being used but well-rotted garden compost, farmyard manure, or bark would serve just as well.

Black polythene is an effective way of conserving soil moisture. Here it is being used around potatoes. Slits are cut to allow the foliage and stems to grow through and no earthing up is required.

Lawn Care

Of all the features in the garden, probably the one capable of making or breaking the whole effect is the lawn. A good one shows off the rest of the garden to perfection and can even improve the appearance of rather indifferent surroundings. On the other hand, a bad one can ruin the whole place, no matter how well everything else is looked after in the garden.

A good lawn does not just happen; it has to be laid down right, whether from seed or from turf, and it has to be cared for properly. Contrary to popular belief, a lawn needs far more attention than any other feature in the garden if it is to look right.

The right start
The ultimate quality of a lawn is determined the moment preparations begin. These should be started well in advance of sowing or turfing so that the ground has plenty of time to settle naturally and weeds can be eliminated. If this preliminary work is skimped or left until the last minute, the result can be a disaster; hills and holes will appear in the lawn in a few months and, if it was seeded, weeds can well choke out the finer grasses. The actual digging and breaking down of the soil and preparing the surface for sowing and turfing are the same as getting it ready for sowing vegetables (see pages 13 and 104).

The choice between seed and turf is largely a matter of cost and when you want the lawn to be usable. Clearly, turf is quicker to establish but more expensive. The quality of the seed or the turf is important because very little can be done once it is down. Except for really high-quality turves, most could be regarded as providing a 'general purpose' lawn and are quite adequate for the average household. They contain a fair proportion of the harder wearing grasses along with fine species to give the lawn 'body'. Much the same applies to seed except that there is a far greater range of mixtures to suit any particular circumstance. It is important to obtain a fine, even tilth before sowing or turfing a lawn. Apply seed evenly at the rate of 40 to 55 g per m^2 (1$\frac{1}{2}$ to 2 oz per sq yd) in April, May or September. Most seed will have already been treated with a bird repellent.

For the best quality cut, there is no doubt that the cylinder type of mower gives the finest results. The cutting height can be reduced to as little as 1 cm (½ in), if required, and, with a front and rear roller, the 'finish' to the lawn is superb.

Hover mowers are excellent where a first-class finish to the lawn is not wanted. They are useful on steeply sloping ground and have the advantage that grass can be cut when wet. Most models have no grass collecting facility, so regular raking is needed to prevent 'thatch'.

Although capable of cutting grass to lawn height, the main use of rotary mowers is for cutting areas of rough grass, such as amongst trees and bushes.

This cord trimmer is a useful machine for cutting grass in awkward places. Here it is being used to tidy up the edge of a lawn alongside a stone step. This is a petrol-driven model but electrical ones are often even handier, and less noisy.

Opposite: A neatly edged lawn sets off brightly coloured bedding plants most effectively

By rights the lawn should be edged as often as it is mown; edging shears provide the most usual and the cheapest method.

Where a lot of edging has to be done, an electric edger is a boon. However, the edges must be well maintained and deep enough to avoid the rotating blades digging into the ground.

An important job in the spring is re-cutting any edges that have become overgrown or uneven during the winter so that edging shears can be used effectively in the coming growing season. Never try to cut straight edges without a plank to guide the half-moon; it only needs one stone to throw the whole thing out of line.

Opposite: A delightful garden can be created in a small space if walls are clothed with climbers and borders carefully planted

Mowing and mowers

Whether a lawn is new or has been in existence for many years, the most time-consuming and important task is going to be mowing. This normally starts in April and should be carried on at regular intervals of about a week until October. However, this should never be thought of as the complete mowing season; if the grass needs cutting, be it June or January, it should be cut, weather permitting.

For the first few mows of the spring and the last ones in the autumn, as well as any during the winter, the height of cut should never be less than about 4 cm ($1\frac{1}{2}$ in). As the frequency of cutting increases, the height can be lowered but, in all but the finest of lawns, it must never be closer than 2 cm ($\frac{3}{4}$ in). As a general rule, the mowings should always be collected or the lawn will eventually suffer from a build-up of dead fibre.

Hot and dry weather during the summer calls for a rather different approach to the lawn. To begin with, the height of cut should be raised so that the grass is not put under even greater strain. It is also the one occasion when it will benefit the lawn if the mowings are not collected as they will tend to act like a blanket and help to prevent excessive evaporation of moisture from the soil.

The choice of mowers is about as varied as the different types of grass available and, similarly, the type you choose depends on what you want it to do.

The basic division is between motor mowers and hand-pushed ones. Obviously, motor mowers are easier to use but they cost a great deal more to buy and have running costs as well. They are really only worthwhile where a lot of mowing is involved. The motive power can be either petrol or electricity.

As regards rotary against cylinder mowers, the cylinder type unquestionably gives you the highest quality finish of any but, here again, they cost more so it mainly rests on the standard of lawn you want.

Feeding the lawn

An essential part of good lawn management is to feed it during the growing season, remembering that it consists of hundreds of thousands of grass plants in intense competition with each other. High-quality lawns will need feeding monthly from about March till September but even the roughest ones should get two feeds a year: one high in nitrogen in the spring and a high potash feed in the autumn. The application of nitrogen will sustain it whilst it is growing and the potash in the autumn will toughen it up for the winter.

There are many lawn fertilizers available and it really is folly to try to economize by using up one that is intended for some other purpose; the saving will be minimal and the results inferior. If possible, always use a spreader to apply lawn fertilizer. It will give the correct application rate and, just as important, it will spread the material evenly.

Several brands of lawn fertilizer incorporate a selective weedkiller and these certainly save time by doing two jobs at once. Their only snag is that, whereas fertilizers on their own are best applied during showery weather, lawn weedkillers work best if it stays dry for a day or two after application. This should always be remembered.

Watering
If it is decided that watering is needed, exactly the same rules should be observed as when watering anything else (see page 25), the most important one being to give a real soaking.

Raking and aerating
The danger of allowing a build-up of dead fibre in the lawn has already been touched on but, inevitably, a certain amount will accumulate during the year. Whilst a little will do no harm, it should never be allowed to get to the stage when the surface is spongy. This is a clear indication that there is a thick layer of 'thatch' present which will lie wet in the winter and act like a macintosh in the summer.

The best way of dealing with thatch is to rake or scarify the lawn vigorously every autumn and again, if you can face it, in the spring. Fortunately there are powered scarifiers for sale or hire nowadays which do an excellent job, so the exhausting task of hand raking can be avoided.

Another problem that can arise in a much used lawn is compaction of the surface soil. Not only will this impede drainage but it will also mean that air cannot penetrate to the roots; both these factors will be to the detriment of the lawn. The answer to this is to spike the surface with a garden fork or special aerator and, although it is far better to tackle the whole lawn, it can, at a pinch, be restricted to the worst affected areas. To do any good, the spiking should be to a depth of at least 10 cm (4 in) with the rows of holes about 10 cm (4 in) apart.

Then top-dress the spiked areas with a 50:50 mix of sifted soil and fine peat or pulverized bark. This provides excellent material for new roots to grow in and will also fill in any slight depressions. If the whole lawn is being top-dressed, the autumn fertilizer can be mixed in, and applied at the same time.

Raking the lawn at least once a year, and preferably twice (spring and autumn), is vital if a build-up of thatch is to be prevented. Thatch, an accumulation of moss, dead grass and other debris, stops rain getting down into the soil in summer and encourages disease by lying wet in the winter.

A much more effective and less exhausting way of raking is to use a mechanical raker. The one illustrated is a mains electric model and is very reasonably priced. Set high it will gather fallen leaves, too.

As well as being raked, a lawn should also be spiked occasionally to counteract compaction and aerate the soil. A perfectly satisfactory way is to drive an ordinary garden fork at least 10 cm (4 in) deep and 10 cm (4 in) apart.

A better method is to use a special spiker or a hollow-tined aerator (illustrated). This is particularly suited for improving badly drained and compacted lawns as it takes out actual cores of soil. These cores of turf are a valuable addition to the compost heap.

Following spiking, especially hollow tining, the lawn will benefit enormously from a top-dressing to fill up the aeration holes and also any slight depressions. It must be worked well into the sward so that the grass is not smothered. A 'lute' (illustrated) is purpose-made for the job but a besom broom works perfectly adequately.

To remove any pronounced hummocks or depressions the turf must be lifted and rolled back. A turfing iron is the best tool for this job. Scrape away soil to level a hump or fill a depression with sifted soil, roll back the turves and firm them well into place.

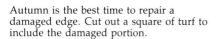

Autumn is the best time to repair a damaged edge. Cut out a square of turf to include the damaged portion.

Slide the square outwards and slice off the ragged bit so that a new straight edge is formed. Fill in the gap left with some sifted soil and re-seed.

Carrying out repairs

Autumn is also the time to carry out any repairs to the lawn, such as making good broken edges, levelling out bumps and filling in holes.

The way to repair edges is clearly shown in the illustrations on page 39. To remove bumps, though, the best system is to lift and roll back the turf, scrape away enough soil from underneath and then replace the turf, firming it back in position. Never try to level a bump by beating it with the back of a spade or by using a heavy roller on it. This will simply cause compaction and create further problems.

Exactly the opposite routine is adopted for coping with sizeable depressions but shallow ones can be corrected by filling them with a top-dressing and working it well into the surface so that none of the grass is smothered.

Pests and diseases

Lawns are usually remarkably free from pests and diseases and, if reasonably well looked after, they may never need any treatment at all.

Some gardeners regard earthworms as pests but it is only their casts that may cause difficulties, and then only on top-quality lawns. In the vast majority of cases, these are nothing more than a tolerable nuisance and can be brushed off. Where control is thought worthwhile, a specific wormkiller based on chlordane is the solution.

The most harmful pests are likely to be leatherjackets, the grubs of the flying daddy-long-legs or crane fly, which feed on the roots of the grass plants. However, even these are really only going to be troublesome on high-quality lawns and an autumn application of wormkiller will take care of them as well.

Moss and weeds

Something that is all too familiar to anyone with a lawn is moss. Space forbids a detailed account of its many causes; suffice it to say that poor drainage, build up of thatch, excessive shade, compaction, too close mowing and under-feeding all play a part, as well as other things. The main thing to remember is that moss is a sure sign that all is not well with the grass. Its control, therefore, must be based on improving conditions so that the grass flourishes. There are many mosskillers on the market, some with fertilizers and some without, but they should always be used in conjunction with improved lawn management or the moss is sure to return.

The other ever-present curse is weeds. Fortunately, unlike moss these are not messengers of disaster but they should, nonetheless, be

In an ordinary household lawn, earthworms cannot really be described as a pest but in a top-quality one their casts can be unsightly and can provide the perfect seed-bed for weeds. Use a besom broom to scatter wormcasts when they are dry.

Although by no means confined to lawns, leatherjackets (the larvae of the crane fly or flying daddy-long-legs) can cause considerable damage by feeding on the roots of the grass; this gives rise to dead and brown patches 2 to 3 cm (about 1 in) across.

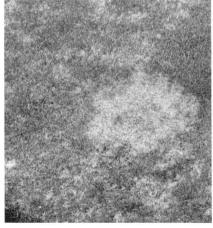

One of the most annoying lawn diseases is fairy ring, though it very seldom actually kills the grass. Toadstools appear in the autumn but the phenomena that immediately identify this disease are the circles of lush grass. Apart from digging up the ground and sterilizing it chemically there is little that can be done.

Fusarium (snow mould) is a disease that normally appears in a damp autumn and sometimes in spring. The grass goes yellowish in small patches which often join up to form larger areas, 30 cm (1 ft) or so across. The grass rarely dies but is severely weakened. Treat with a lawn moss killer/ fungicide based on dichlorophen.

killed before they become too numerous. Not only do they spoil the look of a lawn but they also make it far less hard wearing.

The only way to tackle weeds is to apply a lawn weedkiller. For best results, this should be applied at the height of the growing season during May or June when the weeds will absorb a lethal dose quickly. If some are particularly old and well established, it may be necessary to give a second treatment a month after the first. Where there are only a few, an overall application may not be needed as there are several aerosols and touch-weeders available for individual treatment. Hand weeding is not a good idea as it just creates a patch of bare earth where new weed seeds can settle and germinate.

 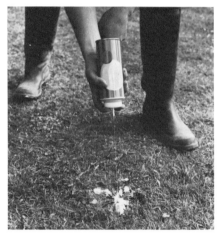

Weeds can ruin the whole look of a lawn and all but the very best carry their fair share. Where weeds are more or less evenly distributed throughout the area, an overall application of lawn weedkiller is called for. This is best applied with a watering-can fitted with a dribble-bar to avoid drift onto surrounding plants.

For isolated weeds, a much more economical way of killing them is to use an aerosol spot-weeder or one of several other similar appliances designed to treat just one weed at a time.

Decorative Plants

One can often find a garden, particularly a small one, where no vegetables are grown or without a lawn but try to picture one without flowers. It hardly bears thinking about. However, it is not always flowers that are the most attractive features of a plant; many are grown for their foliage and others for the colour of their bark. Amongst trees and shrubs, we can find evergreen and deciduous types; plants that climb and those that run along the ground. In fact, it would be hard to find a particular characteristic that at least a handful of plants do not possess.

There are some that we have to grow each year from seed, trees and shrubs which, seemingly, go on for ever, and, between the two, herbaceous perennials which go on from year to year but which die down each winter. If we also consider the different sizes to which plants will grow, it takes little imagination to realize that there is a vast array from which to choose.

Planning, in fact, is probably the most important single consideration and there is a lot more involved than simply buying and growing the plants which appeal to us. One of the first things we have to decide on is whether or not we want to grow vegetables, bearing in mind that, if we do, then we will have to set aside a specific area for them. We also have to consider if we want, or need, a lawn or any hedges and which kinds of decorative plants we would like to put most emphasis on or whether it is to be a good old mixture.

Bulbs, corms and tubers
These are some of the most easily grown and colourful plants in the garden and, with careful choice, there can be something in flower all year round.

First, though, how do the three differ?

All are 'storage organs' in that they contain the energy needed to bring the plant into flower in the following season and to put out fresh roots so that the cycle can be completed. In the case of true bulbs (daffodils, hyacinths, tulips), the energy is stored in the swollen leaf bases of which the whole thing is composed. Corms (crocus and gladioli) work on the same principle except that the storage part is the swollen base of the stem; the brown flakes on the outside are what is left of the leaves. Tubers, for the most part, are swollen roots (dahlias) though there are some vegetables (potatoes) which are underground stems.

The most popular bulbs and corms are undoubtedly the spring-flowering narcissi and crocuses that bring a ray of hope into our lives when all else is usually grey and frozen. They are by no means the only ones though; a quick glance through any bulb catalogue will reveal dozens of different types. Snowdrops, Dutch irises, miniature irises, hyacinths, tulips, grape hyacinths, scillas, anemones, the list is long. These should all be planted in the autumn so that they become well established before the winter and will therefore flower successfully in the spring.

Following on, we have the summer and autumn-flowering ones like gladioli, tuberous-rooted begonias, acidanthera, nerine, lilies, crocosmia and montbretia, St Brigid and De Caen anemones, ranunculus, ornithogalum and a host of others, including all the dahlias. Not all of these are completely hardy but spring planting is perfectly all right. It does raise the question, though, of which ones should be lifted and stored in a frost-free place for the winter. Of those mentioned, gladioli, tuberous begonias and acidanthera are really the only ones that are likely to suffer by being left in the ground and, in very warm and sheltered gardens, it is often safe to leave them, though one is probably going to lose the lot in a very severe winter.

Where to plant? Bulbs can be grown anywhere in the garden from the tiny *Crocus* species, which are perfect for a rockery and for growing in containers, right up to the lilies that grow to 1.2 m (4 ft) and more which are quite at home in shade, unlike many others.

Most bulbs are better in an informal setting but the taller tulip varieties and hyacinths are at their best when interplanted with wallflowers or polyanthus respectively in formal bedding schemes. Avoid planting daffodils and narcissi in these situations; they flower and finish much earlier than the other plants, have too much foliage and need to be left in the ground for longer than is convenient for display bedding.

The need to leave spring-flowering bulbs in the ground after flowering to grow on and mature is most important. If they are denied this period of growth, they get progressively weaker and produce fewer flowers over the years. Similarly, those growing as 'naturalized' bulbs in grass should never have their foliage cut down until it is starting to go yellow.

When naturalizing small groups of bulbs in grass, the best system is to peel back the turf and loosen the underlying soil before planting the bulbs. When all is finished, the turf is folded back and firmed into place.

Naturalizing on a larger scale is best done with a special planter. This takes out a plug of turf to the depth that you want and the bulb is popped into the hole. All that remains is to replace the plug and tread it down.

Lilies are sold complete with their dormant roots as these tend not to die off each year. Therefore, never try to be neat and tidy and cut them off. Plant the bulbs in groups, as shown, and spread the roots well out.

Never tie daffodil foliage up in tasteful little knots; this greatly reduces the efficiency of the leaves. If the growing season is cut short by the removal of the foliage before it yellows, the bulbs are less likely to flower the following year.

Dahlias should be lifted in the autumn as soon as they have been well blackened by the frost. The first step is to cut them down to within about 15 cm (6 in) of the ground; this top growth can go straight on the compost heap.

The tubers are then carefully lifted, labelled and cleaned of loose soil before being stood upside-down in boxes to dry properly for a week or so. After a final cleaning, they should be dusted with sulphur to keep diseases away during storage.

A shallow box with a layer of peat in the bottom is then prepared and the dried tubers are placed in this so that they do not actually touch each other. In this way, if any do go rotten, it is unlikely to spread to neighbours.

Once the box is full, cover the tubers with peat and stand the whole thing in an airy and frost-free place for the winter. In spring the tubers can be started into growth by moistening the peat. When new growth begins the young shoots can be used for cuttings or the tubers divided to provide new plants. Tubers can be planted out in the garden in May.

Annuals and biennials

With the possible exception of bulbs, these are probably the easiest flowers to grow and certainly the quickest to come into flower. They are just the things to start children gardening.

Although there are very few hard and fast rules in nature or gardening, annuals are normally sown in the spring, flower through-out the summer and then die. Biennials differ slightly because, even though they are sown in the spring or summer, they do not flower until the following year.

Annuals can be either hardy (H) or half-hardy (HH). The hardy ones are tough little chaps and can be sown outdoors in the positions in which they are to flower. The half-hardies, though, must be raised in a greenhouse or indoors and are then planted outside towards the end of May when the frosts are over. White alyssum is a good example of a hardy annual (HA), the scarlet bedding salvia of a half-hardy annual (HHA) and wallflowers of a hardy biennial (HB). The letters in brackets are simply what you will see in seed catalogues and on the packets.

Raising from seed   Half-hardy annuals are the earliest to be sown. These should be started in March or early April so that they make strong little plants by the time they are ready for planting out. It always pays to buy a compost specially made for seed sowing to raise them in because garden soil can well contain diseases which will attack the tiny seedlings and kill them. Always sow the seeds thinly in a pot or some other container and cover them lightly with sieved compost to the appropriate depth. Stand the pots in a warm place and bring them into full light the moment the seeds germinate. From then on, they should only be watered when the surface of the compost is drying out. When they are large enough to handle, they will need to be pricked out. This means planting the seedlings singly in pots or seed trays filled with potting compost.

There is no reason why half-hardy annuals should not be sown straight outside but it should be delayed until May or the frost will very likely kill them. Hardy annuals can be sown outdoors as soon as the soil is sufficiently dry in late March or April; some, indeed, may be sown in the previous September and will be the first to flower in the early summer.

The art of growing annuals well is to tread the ground down nice and firmly before sowing them; this stops them growing too strongly and brings them into flower sooner. They should be sown in shallow drills with the recommended distance left between each drill. A useful tip is to sow them in clumps of a few seeds at the right spacing rather than in a continuous line; a packet goes much further this way and there is

When sowing complete borders of hardy annuals, prepare the sowing surface first (see also page 24) and then mark out bold patches with sand to show you where each variety is to be sown. This way, you can make any alterations before it is too late.

Once the pattern is fixed, draw out the actual sowing drills for each patch. Make these so that they do not run from the front of the border to the back or you will see the lines of seedlings for a long while afterwards.

Before pot-sown annuals have become crowded, they should be 'pricked out' into fresh containers of compost and given plenty of room for growth. This will be their last move before they are planted in the open garden.

During the second half of May, the weather should be suitable for them to be planted out. Loosen the compost in the tray by dropping it gently on one edge so that the plants come out quite easily without disturbing the roots too much. Break up the contents of each tray into individual plants either by pulling them apart or, as here, by cutting them with a trowel.

very little waste when they are thinned out later on.

Having sown and shallowly covered the seeds, a good idea is to put netting or twiggy sticks over the border to keep the sparrows off. Given half a chance, the birds will start having dust baths in the fine soil and make a fearful mess. Because biennials are going to be moved later on, they can be sown in a drill somewhere handy. May and June are the best months for sowing. Plant the seedlings out in nursery rows about 23 cm (9 in) each way when they are a few centimetres high to produce good strong plants by the autumn.

Although it is normal to buy herbaceous plants, trees and shrubs as plants, many of them can be raised from seed very successfully. The main snag here is that there can be enormous variation amongst the seedlings but, if this is tolerable, seed is certainly the cheapest way, though it will take a few years for trees and shrubs to reach flowering size.

Herbaceous perennials

The main feature of these is that, although they may only flower for a few weeks each year, they are more or less permanent. Added to this, they take far less work to look after than annuals.

They are usually bought as young plants but growing some types from seed, for example delphiniums, can be great fun as there is no limit to the variability in the resulting plants. They can be raised in the same way as biennials and many will reach flowering size in the following year. Lupins are another good group to try.

Inevitably, even perennials will need rejuvenating after a few years and the normal practice is to carry this out every three or four years. This is to prevent the quality of the plants deteriorating. The best method will vary with the type of plant. We have seen that lupins and delphiniums can be raised from seed but, if a particular strain or variety is to be propagated true to form, they will need to be grown from cuttings taken in the spring. Paeonies, dahlias, geraniums and pinks are also increased in this way. An even more common method is by division as this is suitable for all plants that grow in clumps, like Michaelmas daisies and herbaceous phlox. The time to do this is when the tops have died down in the autumn. Others, and this includes paeonies and phlox again, respond best if they are grown from root cuttings.

Supporting flowers Although the formal bedding plants, like salvias and antirrhinums, are too short and sturdy to require supporting, the same cannot be said for many herbaceous plants and less formal annuals, for example larkspur, love-in-the-mist and the poppies. Left to

Large plants with substantial root systems, such as these wallflowers, should be planted with a trowel and the soil pushed down firmly after planting. Note that the gardener is standing on a board to avoid compacting the soil he is about to plant into.

Exactly the same routine is followed for plants raised in pots except that more care is needed to avoid breaking the root-ball.

In all cases plants should be firmed well down in the soil. In this instance the handle of the trowel does the job.

Opposite: Mixed bulbs – erythroniums, muscari, and narcissi – look charming in an informal grouping

Here are three ways of increasing and improving your stock of herbaceous plants. Many, like Michaelmas daisies, can be split up by pulling the clumps apart. The young portions towards the outside are kept for replanting and the old inside is thrown away.

With plants like lupins, which do not develop in clumps, the best way is to cut the crowns apart with a knife. Make sure that each section has roots and, if possible, dust the cut surfaces with sulphur before replanting to keep fungus diseases away.

These paeonies have thick, fleshy roots and are best dealt with by cutting them into segments with a spade or edging iron. Once again, only the strong outside parts are kept.

Opposite: Taller plants at the back of an herbaceous border will need staking and any dead blooms should be removed regularly ———————

themselves these will be flattened by the first strong wind once they are a few centimetres high.

Although many proprietary gadgets can be bought which do the job well, the cheapest and most natural-looking means is to push twiggy sticks into the ground around them. This should be done immediately after the seedlings have been thinned to the correct distance apart so that the plants grow up amongst the sticks. The height of the sticks should be two-thirds to three-quarters of the ultimate height of the plants so that they are practically invisible, masked by foliage. Really tall subjects will need to have each stem tied individually to a cane.

Over the last twenty years or so, a particularly good system for growing perennials has been devised by Alan Bloom of Bressingham Gardens, the home of modern herbaceous plants. This involves the use of low-growing and sturdy varieties, requiring no staking, which are grown in 'island' beds. This sort of bed differs from the traditional herbaceous border because, having no wall or hedge behind it, it can be viewed from all round.

Tidying up   During the summer, when annuals and perennials are in flower, one of the most important jobs is to keep them 'dead headed' by removing all flowers once they have faded. If these are allowed to remain, they will look very untidy but, more importantly, they are likely to set seed; this will act as a drain on the plants and will drastically curtail their flowering season.

At the end of the season, annuals will, of course, be dug up and thrown onto the compost heap. With perennials, the stalks should be left after flowering until the leaves start to go yellow when they should be cut down and join their companions for making compost.

Most herbaceous plants will need
supporting. This can be done very
effectively with twiggy sticks which should
be pushed into the ground around the
plants shortly after growth has started. As
the plants grow up, the foliage will hide
the sticks.

Even plants that are normally left
unsupported will need attention if they are
at the edge of a border adjoining a lawn.
Here again, twigs are perfectly adequate
and are unobtrusive.

Plants like delphiniums will need some
individual support by tying them to stakes
when they are half-grown. Another tie will
be needed round the flower spike once it is
well above the leaves. It is always best to
put the stake in position early in the season
or straight after planting.

Removing dead flower heads, or 'dead
heading', is an important job with every
flowering plant. Many will have set seed
and a lot of energy will be wasted on seed
production when it should be going
towards more flowers or new growth.

Shrubs and Roses

Shrubs should form the backbone of most gardens as they add an air of permanence. Be sure to select a high proportion of evergreens as these will give interest to otherwise naked borders during the long winter months.

The thought of evergreens usually conjures up a picture of dark green hollies and Victorian laurels and, whilst these are perfectly all right, they can be extremely boring if there are too many of them. Try to use some imagination and bring in as many interesting shrubs as you can. Variegated foliage brings more colour into the garden picture, especially in winter. Keep your eyes open when visiting gardens and nurseries and soon you will have more ideas than you can possibly cope with. Leaves do not have to be brilliantly coloured to be interesting; search out those with an unusual shape. They all add to the charm of the garden.

Contrast should be brought into the borders and, although there needs to be plenty of colour variation, it is just as vital to have variety of form. There are tall thin shrubs, short fat ones and others that grow out along the ground. All have a place in the garden so visit garden centres and, better still, other people's gardens for inspiration.

Conifers

Here again, go for variation. Foliage can be either the traditional dark green or bluish, pale green, golden, yellow and even variegated. You can also find them in virtually any shape you like to think of: columnar, like juniper 'Skyrocket', conical, round, spreading, weeping and even creeping along the ground.

A number only grow to about 60 cm (2 ft) tall, or even less; these are ideal for rockeries whilst the flat ones make marvellous ground cover plants. These should have a place in every garden. Not only do they hide areas of bare soil but they make a grand job of keeping weeds down once they are well established.

Climbers

No garden should be without climbing plants. Not only are they

Planting bare-rooted shrubs

Bare-rooted plants should only be bought during the autumn or winter when they are dormant. If they cannot be planted in their permanent position at once, they must be temporarily heeled in on a spare bit of ground.

When planting a bare-rooted tree or shrub (in this case a rose), a hole is first dug large enough to accommodate the spread-out root system and a fork or plank is laid across the hole to ensure the correct planting depth. This should coincide with the soil mark on the stem.

Some soil is then replaced and the plant is jiggled about to get rid of any air pockets and to work the soil well round the roots.

The replaced soil is then trodden down firmly before the next lot is put in. When all the soil has been replaced, the ground is roughed up to remove compacted footmarks. It is then a good idea to finish off by putting a mulch around the plant (see page 30).

Before planting container-grown shrubs, give them a good watering to ensure that the complete rootball is thoroughly moist.

Dig out the hole for the shrub in the usual way, paying particular attention to the soil in the bottom which must be well broken up to ensure good drainage. With the exception of bitumenized cardboard pots, which can be left in place, all containers must be completely removed before planting to allow the roots to grow out.

Put the shrub in the bottom of the hole, making sure that it is at the right depth, and start putting the soil back.

Firm the soil down with your foot as it is returned but be careful not to disturb the rootball too much or the shrub will take longer to establish.

attractive in their own right but they can also perform the invaluable task of hiding some eyesore or clothing a rather bare wall or fence. Some of the best examples are where climbers have been used to improve further the good looks of an already interesting feature.

Climbers can be either self-clinging, such as ivy, or like clematis, able to hang on to some form of support. Alternatively they may need to be tied to something to stop them simply growing along the ground. Winter jasmine, climbing roses (see page 63) and many of the honeysuckles are of this type.

Ivy is probably one of the best climbers as it has two characteristics that most of us look for in a climber: good looks all year round and the ability to climb completely unaided. What a pity that so many gardeners condemn it, thinking only of the plain green sort. This is most unjust as there is a wealth of variation and many variegated forms, such as *Hedera helix* 'Goldheart' and the more vigorous but not quite so hardy *H. canariensis* 'Gloire de Marengo'. Even amongst the green-leaved forms there is considerable variation in the shades of green, the vigour and the leaf shape. *H. helix* 'Sagittifolia', for example and despite its long name, is a very dwarf plant with the most delicate and deeply cut leaves; it is superb in a rockery where it will adopt a spreading rather than climbing habit.

One myth that must be dispelled about ivy is its effect on bricks and mortar. Only when these are already old and crumbling will it do them the least bit of harm. If the brickwork and pointing are sound, the ivy will, if anything, do some good by keeping the weather off them.

At the other end of the vigour scale, and getting away from ivies, we find the Russian vine, or mile-a-minute (*Polygonum baldschuanicum*). This has to be awarded full marks for sheer effrontery as it will cover an unsightly shed almost faster than you can cut it back; so be warned, because this is probably its only virtue. To be fair, it does have quite attractive heads of tiny white flowers in the autumn, but it is not evergreen.

When choosing climbers, the same consideration should be given as for shrubs in that a good percentage should be evergreen; a plant that loses its leaves in the winter is only of limited value in covering up something hideous until its growth is fairly dense. Conversely, when a climber is being grown up a tree, a deciduous one is going to do far less harm to the 'host' than an evergreen. In many ways, this is the best way to grow climbers as, by choosing the partners carefully, delightful associations can result. One of the prettiest is *Clematis montana rubens* growing in a laburnum tree; the pink and yellow flowers show each other off beautifully in May.

Hydrangea petiolaris makes a lovely sight after a few years and is particularly useful because it is a self-clinging climber that is quite at home on a sunless north wall. It loses its leaves in the winter.

Ivy is one of the finest climbers there is and, today, we certainly do not have to think solely of drab green varieties. *Hedera helix* 'Gold Heart' is an excellent variegated one; so is this grand specimen of *H. canariensis* 'Gloire de Marengo'.

Climbers, even the self-clinging kinds like this clematis, will need regular tying in during their early life until they have covered the area allotted to them. The new shoots will then attach themselves to existing ones.

Climbers that are not self-clinging will need attention throughout their life. The deciduous ones are far easier to deal with in the winter when the leaves are off and the opportunity should also be taken to make sure that existing ties are not too tight.

Heavy snowfalls can be immensely damaging to shrubs; branches will be bent over and can even be broken. The snow must be shaken off the moment it is seen to be causing problems. It often looks pretty but it may ruin the shape of a shrub, particularly a conifer, for ever.

Tender wall shrubs and climbers can be protected very well by covering them with straw or bracken held in place by wire netting and canes. The same system can be used for those growing in the open except that it makes the jobs easier if the shoots are gathered together and loosely tied before covering.

For those who are lucky enough to live where bracken is available, this is one of the finest materials for protecting semi-hardy shrubs in the winter. Make a wigwam of canes around the shrub and use this as a support for the bracken.

In windy situations, young evergreens and conifers can be severely 'burnt' by strong gales or freezing winds in the winter. A piece of sacking or an old sheet will prevent this completely, even if it is a temporary eyesore.

Choosing climbers to grow on a house needs a bit of care. The traditional picture of a cottage in the country with roses round the door is all very well as long as the rose, or anything else for that matter, is not too vigorous. If it is, the choice will lie between continually clipping it away from the windows all summer or needing the lights on the whole time.

Supports With the exception of ivy, the climbing hydrangea and Virginia creeper, all of which are able to cling to flat surfaces, all the most popular climbers will need some form of support up which to climb, for the first few years at any rate.

This support can be natural objects like trees and shrubs or it can be man made, such as trellis work or simply wires fastened to a fence or shed. Never tie the shoots in too tightly to the support or the flow of sap will be cut off as the shoot swells and this can easily lead to its death. Ties should be examined periodically to make sure they have not become too tight. Training in the shoots must be carried out regularly during the growing season, or the autumn will find them all tangled up together and sorting them out will inevitably cause damage.

Wall shrubs

This is by way of a reminder that climbers are not the only plants that can be used to cover up bare spaces. Wall shrubs are really no different to any other shrub, but the ones normally categorized as this perform better with the protection that a wall affords. Indeed, there are several on the borderline of hardiness that need the extra warmth of a wall to flourish, or even survive. Some of the ceanothus need this treatment, along with *Garrya elliptica*.

As a rule, wall shrubs do not have to be tied to anything as most of them are sturdy enough to grow without support but they may need protection in the winter to avoid being damaged by severe frosts.

Mention of frost brings us on to an important precaution that should be taken with all shrubs in the winter. If heavy snowfalls occur, trees and shrubs must be shaken gently to remove the snow or it will easily bend branches out of shape and might even break them. On the other hand, any low-growing plants are usually better off if the snow is allowed to remain as it does provide a measure of protection from the cold and biting winds.

Roses

Roses are rather a special case amongst shrubby plants because the popular hybrid tea (large-flowered bush roses) and floribunda (cluster-flowered bush roses) types are essentially formal plants that are shown to best advantage when massed together in beds. There are, however, plenty of others to choose from; climbers and ramblers, the old-fashioned shrub roses and, possibly the best of all, the mainly wild rose species.

Bush roses   The reason for hybrid teas and floribundas looking best when grouped together is that, as even the most ardent devotee must admit, they do look rather like a lot of upturned chairs in the winter; this immediately puts them at a disadvantage in a mixed border. During the summer, though, they more than justify themselves by giving us a blaze of colour from June until the early winter.

The two types differ in that the hybrid teas produce a smaller number of flowers but each one is larger and, in some eyes, the perfect rose. Floribundas have more flowers of smaller size and rely on their mass effect rather than individual blooms. This difference is catered for in the pruning which should be more severe for the hybrid teas (see page 69).

Climbing roses   These obviously have a totally different growth habit but, in many respects, their flowers are very similar to the bush varieties. Indeed, many of them are simply vigorous mutations (sports) of hybrid teas and floribundas. Although they are described as 'climbing', this should not be taken too literally as they will certainly need to be trained and tied in when grown against a fence or wall. However, if they are planted at the base of an old apple tree that is well past its best, they will scramble about amongst the branches completely unaided after the initial tying and training. This is one of the finest ways of growing them.

Pruning climbers is largely a matter of encouraging them to cover their allotted space as quickly as possible (see page 70). Thereafter, they can be kept tidy and vigorous by the occasional removal of the oldest stems and by shortening back or tying in the side shoots.

Ramblers   These are often confused with, and treated like, climbers but are, in fact, a distinct group on their own. This is because, unlike climbers, most varieties send up plenty of new shoots from the base each year and it is these which give the best flowers in the following summer. Climbers flower better on side shoots that develop on the main stems and send up very few, if any, new shoots from the base.

Another difference is that the ramblers' flowering period is much shorter and is usually confined to an all-out effort in midsummer. This gives us a reliable clue as to the best way of pruning them (see page 71). Whereas the previous types should be tidied up in November and then pruned properly in March, ramblers are best dealt with as soon as they have finished flowering so that the new stems have every chance to grow unhindered.

Shrub roses   A group of roses that is fast becoming popular again are the so-called 'shrub' roses. These are some of the oldest of all cultivated roses and require less attention than those already dealt with. The older varieties tend to produce fewer flowers and over a shorter period than many gardeners would like but new ones have been introduced which have largely overcome this. Many of them have very spiny shoots and the flowers are recognized by their many petals. As with all other types, their scent is variable. Little or no pruning is required beyond keeping the bushes tidy and occasionally removing shoots that have become old and worn out.

Species roses   This is a very important group, and in many respects the finest. These are either naturally occurring types from various parts of the world or improvements on them. There are, of course, hybrids as well. The range of flower colours and habits of growth are vast, from little ones that hug the ground right up to *Rosa banksiae* which is capable of climbing to 6 m (20 ft) or more.

Between these comes a huge array of shrubby species, many of which carry spectacular hips in the autumn; *Rosa moyesii* 'Geranium' is one of the best for these. Decorative thorns are also a feature of a number of them.

Their variability might lead one to think that pruning is complicated. Far from it; the vast majority can be left almost entirely alone and require no more attention than the shrub roses.

Mention has already been made of dead-heading flowers when they fade and this is nowhere more important than with roses, except for those that produce showy hips, of course. If the flowers are left, most will form uninteresting hips which are not worth having and which will greatly weaken the bush and restrict the number of flowers produced later in the season.

Pruning decorative plants

Aspects of this subject have already cropped up under the various types of decorative plants, and fruit will be dealt with specifically in the appropriate section. Here, though, we will look at the 'dos and don'ts' of pruning in general. It will be found that once the general principles are understood, the subject becomes far less mysterious and daunting.

The main purpose of pruning any plant is to keep it to the shape and size that you want it to be. With roses and other flowering plants, there is the additional reason that correct pruning will greatly increase the quantity and quality of the flowers. Much the same applies to fruit trees and bushes and, with these, we have to remember that a good crop is really what we are after. The right kind of pruning will not only ensure this but it will also help to prevent overcropping and a consequent drop in quality. But, first, a few words about the tools that we will be using.

Tools   The main pruning tool is a good pair of secateurs. 'Good' means that they must be strong and reliable. There are several first rate makes on the market which, if looked after, will last a lifetime. Keep them sharp at all times, free from rust and occasionally oiled.

Secateurs should not be used to cut branches thicker than about 2.5 cm (1 in) in diameter; for these, long-handled loppers are recommended. A good pair will easily cut through branches up to 4 cm (1½ in) in diameter and are particularly useful for removing shrub branches at ground level as they will fit into places not convenient for a saw.

For larger branches a pruning saw must be used. There are many makes available but all have one feature in common: the blades are narrow so that they will fit into almost anywhere. A particularly good one is a pruning saw which folds up like a pocket knife and, instead of the teeth being off-set, the blade is thinner along the back edge than along the cutting edge, resulting in a very much smoother cut.

Whilst a proper gardening knife is not essential, it is certainly useful for smoothing saw cuts and you will find many other uses for it other than connected with pruning. It *must* be sharp; a blunt knife is worse than useless.

When to prune   The question often arises as to when is the best time of year to prune. This is something that cannot be answered in a word because it all depends on why you are pruning. As a general rule, fruit trees and bushes are best dealt with as soon as the leaves have fallen in the autumn but, really, any time during the dormant season is quite safe. The main exception to this is with plums which should be left until just before they begin to grow in the spring.

Ornamentals grown for their foliage, both evergreen and deciduous, can also be pruned then but with flowering shrubs, the case is slightly different. Flowering shrubs are of two basic types: those that flower before midsummer on shoots that grew in the previous year and those that flower later in the summer on shoots of the current season's growth.

The first group, shrubs such as forsythia and philadelphus, should be pruned straight after flowering so that the maximum amount of time is allowed for next year's flowering shoots to develop.

The later flowering ones, like bush and climbing roses and the summer-flowering clematis, must be pruned before growth starts in the spring to give the greatest time for the new shoots to grow. This all boils down to one simple fact: if you are at a loss to know when to prune a shrub, wait until it flowers. That will provide the answer in the vast majority of cases.

The rules of pruning These are simple and largely a matter of common sense. When pruning a young shoot, always cut to a bud that is pointing in the direction in which you want that shoot to grow.

Whatever tool is being used, never leave a snag of wood like a coat hook. It serves no useful purpose and will often become infected by fungus diseases.

All saw cuts should be treated with a special pruning paint after they have been pared smooth with a knife. 'Seal and Heal' is one of the best – it is based on latex, contains a fungicide and the brush can be cleaned in water.

Try not to prune during frosty weather as this may lead to the death of the terminal bud.

Secateurs and loppers should be used with the non-cutting blade on the outside of the cut so that the bark is not crushed on the 'tree' side. The picture shows this better than words. Finally, never cut out a branch or shoot simply for the sake of doing so; always remove it for a definite reason.

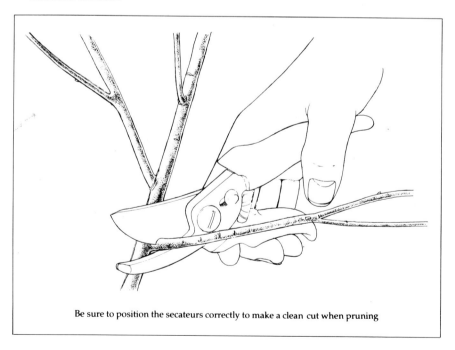

Be sure to position the secateurs correctly to make a clean cut when pruning

Pruning shrubs

When pruning to a bud, always do it correctly; the one on the left has too long a snag and this will often die back and spread below the bud. The next three shoots along have all been pruned too close to the bud which is unlikely to grow out as it may well be frosted. The fifth shoot has been cut at a bad angle and, here again, die-back could well occur. Only the shoot on the far right has been pruned correctly.

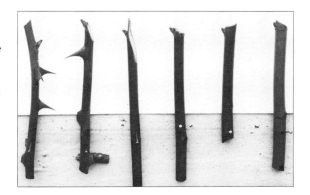

Die-back, the result of bad pruning, should be completely cut out as soon as it is noticed.

The amount of pruning required by shrubs varies enormously according to what they are. For example, buddleia should be cut hard back in the early spring to encourage strong new flowering shoots.

Broom, on the other hand, should never be pruned hard as new shoots are very shy to appear from old wood and die-back can occur. Aim at preventing the bush from becoming too leggy by removing a few of the highest shoots after they have flowered. Beyond this, a little judicial thinning is all that is normally needed.

The only pruning that many shrubs will require is the removal of shoots or branches that are clearly growing out of place or causing overcrowding. Some, however, like forsythia, should also have the oldest branches cut out after flowering to encourage new shoots to develop as it is these that produce the best flowers.

Wistaria is rather a special case in that the first job is to build a framework of permanent branches. Thereafter, the long shoots produced each year are cut back to about 15 cm (6 in) in July.

They are then pruned to two or three buds in the winter. This encourages a spur system which will flower far more freely than a tree that has been left alone. These pictures show a magnificent specimen before and after winter pruning.

Heathers (ericas) are best pruned in the early spring soon after growth starts. The easiest way to keep them thick and bushy is certainly to use shears.

A bush rose, in this case a floribunda or cluster-flowered bush, ready for heading back in October.

The same bush after heading back. Note that proper pruning does not take place yet; the bush has merely been tidied up and the longest shoots shortened so that the inevitable winter winds do not rock it around.

In March pruning proper can take place. Remember all cuts should be made to a bud facing outwards so that the resulting growth creates a nice open bush.

After pruning, all weak shoots should have been removed and strong ones shortened. Although this bush is a floribunda, it has been pruned rather harder than normal because it is an exposed site. Hybrid teas are treated in exactly this way. In a more sheltered site floribundas can be pruned rather less drastically.

A standard rose is headed back in October to tidy it up for the winter as described for the bush roses. Proper pruning takes place in March when the head is thinned out by removing badly placed and crossing shoots together with any weak or unproductive ones. The remainder are shortened back to two or three buds.

In this way a virtual new bush is allowed to form each year. This ensures plenty of flowers and not too much growth, which could result in top-heaviness. Check the tie regularly to make sure that it is not too tight, too loose or wearing out.

Climbing roses can usually be pruned properly in October because the extra warmth provided by a wall is normally enough to keep the worst of the cold off them. The main long growths have been retained but the side shoots have been shortened back to about 15 cm (6 in) before tying in to the supports.

A rambler rose should be pruned as soon as the flowers have faded in the summer to encourage the production of strong new flowering shoots. First cut the rose free of its support. Most of the shoots which have flowered are then cut back to the ground but, where a variety fails to produce enough new shoots, it may be necessary to retain a few of the old ones.

If this is the case remove those side shoots which have flowered, leaving the others to flower the next year.

When pruning is complete, all those shoots remaining are tied back to their support.

Although not strictly pruning, the removal of rose suckers is an important task if the plant is not to be robbed of much of its energy. They should not be cut off at soil level but pulled off cleanly from their point of origin.

HEDGES

Hedges can enhance or ruin a garden; it all depends on what they are and how well they are looked after. They have three main uses. To provide a boundary along a road or between gardens; to split up a garden internally so that there is a definite break between its different sections and to provide shelter from strong winds.

Choosing a suitable type is far from easy; there is probably no such thing as the perfect hedge. What we all want is something that will grow fast until it reaches the desired height and then stops. If we can avoid clipping it, so much the better; it must smother weeds but not encroach into the garden or need fertilizers. It must be decorative all the year round and, if possible, impenetrable. Finally, it would be good if it had fruits or berries in the autumn that could be eaten or sold; surely this is not asking too much?

Although no plant has all these virtues, many have some of them so the choice boils down to the ones that come nearest to what we want. Whatever the purpose of a hedge, it will have to be either formal or informal, and, clearly, the plant you choose will be dependent upon this.

A formal hedge usually takes up less room but will need clipping at least twice a year to retain its rigid lines and shape. An informal one will also need to be clipped or pruned annually but, beyond this, it is normally left to grow at will. A windbreak will have to be shaped in its early years but will need little attention after that.

Probably the greatest mistakes made by gardeners are as follows:
(a) To put the individual plants in too close.
(b) To use too vigorous a species.
(c) To sacrifice shape for the sake of height.
(d) To ignore the fact that *all* plants need regular feeding.

The speed of growth is a point to consider. Everyone wants a hedge quickly but it must be remembered that the fastest growers will also make the tallest hedges. For example, one of the best hedging plants is the Leyland Cypress but any attempt to restrict this to less than about 2.5 m (8 ft) tall is doomed from the start.

There are so many plants suitable for growing as hedges that it is impossible to list them all but a few suggestions are given in the table opposite.

Clipping Apart from the other points mentioned, probably the most important, and perplexing, is clipping.

The time when most attention is needed is during the first three years or so when the foundation is being laid down. The young plants will probably need to be pruned rather than clipped, three or four

GOOD HEDGING PLANTS

Variety	Type	Height	Foliage	Planting distance
Beech *(Fagus)*	formal	1.5 m (5 ft)	dead leaves kept in winter	30–45 cm (1–1½ ft)
Holly *(Ilex)*	formal	1.5 m (5 ft)	evergreen	45 cm (1½ ft)
Leyland's Cypress	formal or informal	2.5 m (8 ft)	conifer	75 cm–1.1 m (2½–3½ ft)
Lonicera nitida	formal	Up to 1.2 m (4 ft)	usually evergreen	30–38 cm (1–1½ ft)
Privet *(Ligustrum)*	formal	1.2 m (4 ft)	evergreen	30–45 cm (1–1½ ft)
Yew *(Taxus)*	formal	1.2 m (4 ft)	conifer	45–60 cm (1½–2 ft)

INFORMAL AND DECORATIVE

	Attraction		Foliage	Planting distance
Berberis stenophylla	yellow flowers	2 m (6 ft)	dark green evergreen	45 cm (1½ ft)
Chaenomeles	orange/red flowers. Fruit	1.5–2 m (5–6 ft)	deciduous (D)	45–60 cm (1½–2 ft)
Escallonia	red/pink/white flowers	1.5–2 m (5–6 ft)	evergreen	60 cm–1 m (2–3 ft)
Pyracantha	flowers and berries	1.5–2 m (5–6 ft)	evergreen	60 cm (2 ft)

SUITABLE ROSES

	Flower colour		Hips	
'Chinatown'	yellow with pink edges	1.2–1 m (4–5 ft)	no	75 cm (2½ ft)
'Queen Elizabeth'	pink	2–2.1 m (6–7 ft)	no	75 cm (2½ ft)
'Penelope'	semi-double creamy pink	1.2–1.5 m (4–5 ft)	yes	1 m (3 ft)
Rosa moyesii	vermilion	2.5–3 m (8–10 ft)	yes	1 m (3 ft)
Rosa rugosa	white, pink, red	1.2–1.5 m (4–5 ft)	yes	1 m (3 ft)
Sweetbrier *(R. eglanteria R. rubiginosa)*	pink	1.2–1.5 m (4–5 ft)	yes	75 cm (2½ ft)
'Zéphirine Drouhin'	double pink	1.5–2 m (5–6 ft)	no, thornless	1 m (3 ft)

times a year at this stage so that a thick, well-furnished basis results.

After that, formal hedges should be clipped twice a year, in May and August. Informal hedges, except roses, which are pruned at their usual times, are normally dealt with after flowering and rather harder than if they were free-standing shrubs. This means more shoots than usual will need to be cut out to keep the hedge tidy. It may even be necessary to prune spring-flowering subjects again in the summer if any shoots are growing too long. When clipping or pruning any hedge, bear in mind that the base will stay much fuller if it is encouraged to grow wider than the top. Obviously this should not be carried too far but the aim should be to create a slight wedge shape so that the base is as well furnished with shoots and leaves as the top.

When plants with large leaves, like the laurel, are grown as a hedge, they must never be clipped with shears but pruned with secateurs. This avoids cutting the leaves in half, which always looks untidy and frequently leads to the browning or death of that particular leaf.

With hedges that shed their leaves in the autumn, a good tip is to run some wire netting along each side at ground level when the first ones start to fall. This stops them being blown all over the garden. They can either be left as a mulch or collected and put on the compost heap.

Evergreens with large leaves should be pruned with secateurs, rather than clipped with shears, to avoid any leaves being cut and consequently dying

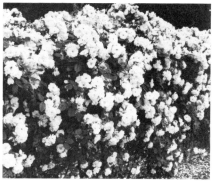

Some of the best informal hedges are grown from members of the genus *Berberis*. Most have flowers followed by berries in the autumn and all are prickly to varying degrees. Both deciduous and evergreen species are available and the leaves can range in colour from purple to dark green.

Surely the ideal hedge – decorative for a long time in the summer, quick growing and armed with thorns that make it virtually impenetrable. This rose is 'Penelope' but many others are suitable with *Rosa rugosa* and its cultivars probably coming top of the list for cheapness.

By no means suitable, or possible, for all gardens, yew is one of the finest plants for formal hedging as it can be clipped into more or less any shape you wish. Here, the completely natural background of woodland provides a magnificent contrast to the rigid lines of the hedge.

When a hedge, particularly a conifer, has reached the required height, the top of each plant should be taken out. To make sure that the result is level, a line is stretched tight along the hedge at the desired height to act as a guide.

Vigorous hedges like privet will need clipping several times during the growing season if they are to be kept tight and dense with plenty of leaves. When clipping the sides, a better hedge is formed if the top is slightly narrower than the bottom.

Depending on its height, the top of a hedge can be clipped either from the ground or by standing on something, whichever is most comfortable. The shears can be used in different ways according to the height of the work.

An electric hedge trimmer is a boon if a lot of hedges or a considerable length have to be cut but, it must be admitted, it is rather an expensive luxury in small gardens. When using one, be careful that neither it nor your enthusiasm runs away with you; only cut as much as is needed.

Undeniably, the most labour-saving way of maintaining a hedge is to treat it with a growth inhibitor like Cutlass. As you can see, it reduces growth to a minimum without spoiling the quality of the hedge. One clipping followed by treatment in the late spring will keep hedges in shape for the rest of the year.

Opposite: Heathers and conifers look attractive all the year round and, when established, require minimal maintenance

Growing Fruit

Growing fruit in gardens really should be more popular. In the case of tree or top fruits (apples, pears, plums, cherries), there are few other plants which are able to boast of beautiful flowers in the spring, decorative fruitlets in the summer, and large, attractive and edible crops in the autumn.

TREE FRUITS

All the popular types of fruit are easy to grow in a garden and even things like peaches, nectarines, apricots and figs present few problems.

Possibly the thing that puts people off growing fruit, particularly trees, is the amount of room that they take up. This belief is based largely on ignorance because there are trees available in so many shapes and sizes that there is bound to be one for even the smallest garden. Let us look at this aspect right away so that the myth is exploded from the start.

Tree forms

Small trees are becoming increasingly popular with the little gardens of today so we will start at the bottom and work up in size.

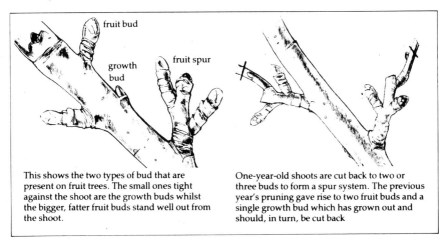

This shows the two types of bud that are present on fruit trees. The small ones tight against the shoot are the growth buds whilst the bigger, fatter fruit buds stand well out from the shoot.

One-year-old shoots are cut back to two or three buds to form a spur system. The previous year's pruning gave rise to two fruit buds and a single growth bud which has grown out and should, in turn, be cut back

Opposite: The stunning rose 'Handel' trained against a wall. Along with other climbing roses it should be pruned in October

Cordons   Apart from those grown in tubs, which is quite possible, cordons are the smallest of the tree forms and are suitable for apples and pears. They can be planted as little as 1 m (3 ft) apart and are grown at an angle of 45° to make them more fruitful. Their tops should be pointing towards the north. Each tree consists of a single stem which bears fruiting spurs instead of branches. Summer and winter pruning are necessary if they are to give of their best and they have to be trained to a cane and wire support to keep them straight. Cordons can be grown in the open ground or trained against a wall or fence.

Espaliers   These take longer to form than cordons but fewer trees are needed to fill a given space. They are suitable for growing apples and pears. Each tree has a central stem from which horizontal tiers of branches grow. 3.7 to 6 m (12 to 20 ft) must be allowed between trees, the actual distance being dependent on the vigour of the variety and rootstock and the nature of the soil. Wires will be needed to which to train the branches and these should be 30 to 38 cm (12 to 15 in) apart and strained tight.

Fan-trained trees   Although these are primarily for stone fruits (plums, peaches, cherries), apples and pears can also be grown as fans, the trees being trained either in the open garden or against a wall. Horizontal wires should be spaced 23 cm (9 in) apart and extend to at least 2.1 m (7 ft) high. Work out the distance to allow between trees on the basis of each one requiring at least 18 m^2 (194 sq ft). Divide this by the height to which the tree is to grow to find the distance apart. Unlike the espalier, the branches of the fan tree radiate out from a short trunk like the rays of a fan.

Dwarf pyramids   This is the smallest type of tree that does not need to be trained to wires. Apples, pears and plums can all be grown as dwarf pyramids but whereas apples and pears will only need to be 1 to 1.2 m (3 to 4 ft) apart, plums should be 2.1 to 3.7 m (7 to 12 ft) according to the rootstock being used; more of this later. Although summer pruning is not essential, a better control over the trees will be possible if this is carried out in conjunction with winter pruning.

Bush trees   Unlike the previous forms, these really do look like trees but are kept relatively small by the choice of rootstock and a short trunk of only about 60 cm (2 ft) high. Even so, they make quite large trees and 2.5 m (8 ft) should be regarded as the minimum distance between them and up to 6 m (20 ft) may be needed, depending on the type of fruit, the variety and the rootstock. All tree fruits can be grown as bush trees and only winter pruning is necessary.

Half-standards   These grow larger than bush trees and are really only suitable for larger gardens where they can be grown as specimen trees either in mixed borders or in the lawn. The 1.2- to 1.5-m (4- to 5 ft) trunk makes it easy to work under them. All fruits can be grown as half-standards but, because of their size, around 6 m (20 ft) will be needed between them. Here again, only winter pruning is needed.

Other tree forms Although those described above are the main ones that gardeners are likely to be concerned with, several other tree forms exist which are perfectly satisfactory though, it must be said, they seldom offer advantages over the others. A probable exception to this is a method of training called 'festooning' which was developed at Highfield Nurseries, Whitminster, Gloucestershire.

It involves bending the season's new shoots down and tying them in the autumn so that they grow less vigorously and fruit much sooner. It is simple and quick to carry out and obviously has many advantages.

Commercial growers often train trees as 'spindles'. These stay quite small and are easy to manage but they do look rather untidy. The traditional 'standard' trees, older specimens of which are still found in some gardens, are really far too large and difficult to look after.

Rootstocks

Fruit trees are not grown from cuttings, but the variety required is budded or grafted onto a readymade set of roots known as the rootstock. This is done for two main reasons. The first is that it is the easiest way for nurserymen to propagate fruit trees. The second, and even more important, is that the rootstock will determine the ultimate size of the tree, its vigour and how soon it starts cropping.

Because apples are a most popular tree fruit, both commercially and in gardens, there is a very wide choice of rootstocks which provide us with a more or less unlimited variety of tree sizes. The four of particular interest to gardeners are as follows.

M (Malling) 27 This produces the smallest of all trees and is suitable for cordons, dwarf pyramids and bush trees. It is also excellent for trees grown in pots. Apples grown on M 27 crop very early in their life (two to four years old) and bush trees require virtually no pruning after the first five years or so. It should only be used on very fertile land and trees will need to be staked throughout their life.

M 9 Trees on this very dwarfing stock are about twice the size of those on M 27 but are still very small compared with ordinary trees. Good soil is again required if the trees are to be a success and, under most circumstances, this is the most dwarfing stock that should be used. Its uses are the same as M 27 and all trees will need support.

M 26 Described as semi-dwarfing, this is the best one to have for a small tree on land that is not too good.

Oblique cordons are pruned in summer as this channels their energy into producing fruit buds. In winter, all new shoots growing from the main stem are cut back to 8 cm (3 in) and all those growing from spurs to 2.5 cm (1 in). To encourage side shoots, the leader may be cut back by one third.

An espalier in winter after pruning. This is an excellent method of training apples or pears. If a dwarfing rootstock such as M9 is used, they can be kept very compact, though they are often seen much larger.

A young espalier tree in mid-July ready for summer pruning. The tree is somewhat cramped at the moment but there is plenty of room above for it to spread in years to come.

The same tree after summer pruning. The extension growth on the central stem has been left and suitably placed shoots have been tied down to form more horizontal branches. All others have been cut back to 8 cm (3 in).

Fan-trained trees are a better method of training stone fruits like plums, peaches and cherries. Here the tree is protected from the attentions of birds with a fruit cage (see page 102).

Although this bush tree is in a commercial orchard, it gives a good idea of the sort of size you can expect them to grow in a garden. Preventing them from growing too high by suitable pruning is an important part of their management. It is being grown on an MM 106 rootstock. (See page 80.)

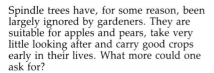

Spindle trees have, for some reason, been largely ignored by gardeners. They are suitable for apples and pears, take very little looking after and carry good crops early in their lives. What more could one ask for?

The crucial time for fruit is during flowering when the blossom is particularly susceptible to frost damage. An effective protection for small trees and wall-trained specimens is to cover them overnight with old sheets, hessian or even polythene sheeting whenever there is a frost warning.

Remove large branches in two operations. First cut off the greater part of the branch but leave a snag a few centimetres long, then saw off this snag flush with the trunk.

This will avoid the problem of a branch falling and tearing off a strip of bark. Any damage like this provides an entry point for diseases.

After removing the branch, pare the edges of the wound clean with a sharp knife and treat the cut surface with a sealant like Seal and Heal or Arbrex; this will speed up the healing process and prevent fungal infection from entering.

A long-arm pruner is invaluable when pruning trees. Although ornamentals seldom need enough attention to warrant buying one, fruit trees are a very different matter as one often wants to stop them getting too tall.

In the renewal system of pruning apple and pear trees the aim is to produce a succession of smallish fruiting branches. The oldest of these are cut out to make room for new ones when they are either too large, out of place or simply no longer fruitful. The old leader shown is not ready to come out yet but the replacement is being built up for the time when it is.

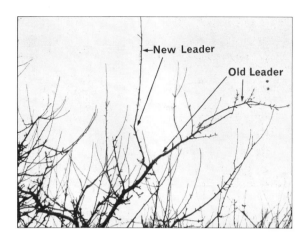

How to renovate an old and neglected fruit tree, in this case an apple, is a common enough problem, especially in a newly acquired garden.

Start by thinning out the head by removing a few large and key branches rather than a lot of snipping about with secateurs. More detailed work will be carried out later on when the tree has started growing again and produced some new wood. The renewal system of pruning can then be followed.

Peaches, nectarines and apricots, whether grown outdoors or in a greenhouse, should be fan-trained against a grid like the one in the picture. As fruits are only produced on shoots that grew in the previous year, as many of these as can be kept without overcrowding should be tied in and, where too long, cut back to a convenient length.

Fan-trained trees should have their new shoots thinned in May so that those left are about 15 cm (6 in) apart along both the upper and lower surface of the branches.

Summer pruning of other trained fruit trees, such as cordons and espaliers, greatly encourages the formation of fruit buds. This is carried out when the current season's shoots have hardened at the base, usually in late July or August. They are cut back to 8 cm (3 in) if they are growing directly from a branch or 2.5 cm (1 in) when on a previously pruned shoot or spur.

MM 106   By far the most commonly used rootstock and suitable for apple trees of every shape and size except very small ones.

The choice of rootstocks for pears is much more limited; in fact there are only two and they are both selected from quince seedlings.

Quince A   This is the most commonly found and is suitable for all tree forms. It is, though, inclined to be rather vigorous on good soil but one is often not given the choice of an alternative.

Quince C   Less vigorous than Quince A but not widely used as yet; until quite recently, virus disease was a problem. It is suitable for all tree forms and should certainly be sought if you do not want a tree that gets too large or difficult to manage.

There are also only two plum rootstocks and, as with pears, one of them dominates the scene.

St Julien A   Often the only one available. It is quite suitable for bush and dwarf pyramids though is, perhaps, rather strong for fan trees on good soil. It is also the stock used for peaches, nectarines and apricots.

Pixy   Within the last few years this semi-dwarfing stock has become available. It is certainly the best one for gardens as it produces a tree two-thirds the size of those on St Julien A. All good nurserymen are now using them both. Unfortunately, it is only suitable for plums.

Colt   Although cherries have not been mentioned before, there is now this rootstock for them which is of similar vigour to Pixy. No attempt should be made to grow cherries on any other stock in gardens as the resulting trees will be far too large.

Regarding rootstocks in general, buying a tree on a specific one is not always easy and, where the one of your choice is not available, the manager of the nursery or garden centre should always be consulted so that an appropriate substitute can be found. Their local knowledge will ensure that you get the right one for the job.

Types and varieties

On the whole, gardeners are very conservative people and this probably accounts for the fact that, over the last one hundred years, the two apple and two pear varieties most commonly grown have remained unchanged: Cox's Orange Pippin (dessert) and Bramley's Seedling (cooker) for apples and Conference and Comice pears. This is a great pity because only one of the four, Conference pear, can really be recommended unreservedly for gardens. Cox and Comice are unreliable croppers and Bramley makes much too large a tree. Granted, all three are probably the best varieties of their type for flavour but it seems a shame to sacrifice all else for this.

Here are some varieties of the different types of tree fruit, every one of which can be recommended for gardens. All are normally reliable croppers and have no serious faults, unless specifically mentioned. Above all, every one has good flavour.

Apples (dessert)
Discovery – August/September; good colour.
Fortune – September/October; striped with red.
St Edmund's Pippin – September/October; heavy russet.
Greensleeves – new variety; October/November; green to yellow.
Sunset – November/December; similar to Cox; well coloured.
Spartan – October/January; dark red; excellent flavour.
Jupiter – new variety; October/January; similar to Cox.
Ashmead's Kernel – December/March; coloured with medium russet.
Norfolk Royal Russet – new variety; October/January; good colour; medium russet.
Apples (cooking)
Early Victoria – July/August; medium sized; green.
Golden Noble – September/January; medium sized; green to yellow.
Grenadier – August; medium to large; slight colour.
Lane's Prince Albert – January/March; coloured; small and compact tree.
Bramley's Seedling – November/March; very vigorous; the best cooker.
Pears (dessert)
Beth – September; yellow tinged with red.
Onward – new variety; late September; red flushed.
Merton Pride – September/October; green to yellow.
Conference – October/November; green to yellow.
Comice – November; yellow, sometimes red flush; possibly the best flavour.
Winter Nelis – November/December; green to yellow.
Pears (cooking)
Catillac – October/April; green with reddish flush.
Plums
Victoria – mid-August; bright red; dual purpose.
Denniston's Superb – mid-August; green; dessert.
Cambridge Gage – late August; green; dessert.
Jefferson – early September; green/yellow; dessert.
Coe's Golden Drop – September/October; yellow; dessert.
Czar – early August; purple; cooker.
Farleigh Damson – mid-September; purple; cooker.
Shropshire Prune Damson – September/October; purple; cooker.

Cherries
Morello – Dark red; self-fertile; cooker.
Stella – Dark red; self-fertile; dessert.
Peaches
Peregrine – early August; the best for flavour.
Rochester – early August; the easiest to grow.
Both will grow well outdoors but are best trained to a sunny wall or fence.
Nectarines
Elruge – late August.
Lord Napier – early August.
These should also be grown on a wall and are less hardy than peaches.
Apricots
Moorpark – August.
Apricots also need the protection of a wall.

Pollination
Without going too deeply into the sex life of fruit trees, it must be appreciated that all types will only give maximum crops if they have been pollinated by bees and other insects at flowering time by another variety of the same kind of fruit. Some varieties are self-fertile; these will carry a crop when fertilized by their own pollen but it will not be particularly heavy. Self compatible means the same thing. Stella cherry and Conference pear are typical examples.

The three most important requirements for successful pollination are good weather at flowering time, a sufficient overlap of flowering periods of the varieties designed to pollinate each other and fertile pollen. The weather is largely out of our hands, though we can do something to protect small trees from night frosts. A good overlap of flowering times can be achieved at planting if only suitable varieties are bought. In addition, many nursery lists actually recommend varieties which are reliable pollinators for others.

Fertile pollen may sound rather beyond us but a peculiarity of some varieties is that their pollen is sterile, or nearly so, and useless for pollination. This applies to Bramley and Jupiter apples. If you plan to grow either of these, there should be at least two other varieties close by so that they will pollinate each other as well as the sterile variety. A sterile variety will be described as 'triploid' in varietal lists. Just because cross-pollination is a virtual necessity, you should not assume automatically that two varieties will need to be bought at a time; this may be so but it could equally well be that a tree in a neighbouring garden will do the job adequately. This is well worth checking on.

Storage

Although most tree fruits will keep for a short time after picking, the only ones that will store successfully are certain varieties of apples and pears. There is no clear dividing line between those that should be eaten or cooked straight off the tree and those that may be stored to mature later but, as a guide, those that will mature in November and afterwards can normally be stored until the last month mentioned in the list on page 88. For example, Conference and Comice pears can be stored until about the end of November.

There are several methods of storing apples and probably the most convenient is to wrap each fruit in newspaper, place it in a cardboard or wooden box and keep this in as cool, but frost free, a place as possible.

Apples can be stored successfully for several months if they are individually wrapped in newspaper or special wrappers

For smaller quantities, they can be put unwrapped into polythene bags with the tops just folded under and not sealed. The bags then go into a similarly cool place. An advantage of this method is that less moisture is lost and fruits do not become shrivelled and woolly. Pears need more air around them when stored so the best system is to put them unwrapped into tomato trays or simply lay them out on shelves.

One very important thing about storage is that fruits should be completely sound and quite free from damage or disease. Under certain conditions, it may also be necessary to protect them from mice.

SOFT FRUITS

In this category we include strawberries, raspberries, blackberries, tayberries and the other hybrids, gooseberries, red currants and blackcurrants. All are easy to grow in gardens and most will take up no more room than a row of vegetables; some, in fact, will take up less as they can be grown against walls or fences. Their cropping life will last for anything from three years for strawberries to about 12 for cane fruits (raspberries, blackberries) and up to 15 for bush fruits (currants and gooseberries).

A great virtue that most soft fruits have is that they can be deep frozen, so gone are the days of coping with a glut.

Added to this, we now have earlier and later varieties that greatly extend the natural season. There are even autumn-fruiting raspberries and strawberries that keep cropping until the frosts arrive. At the other end of the season, cloches or polythene tunnels can be used to advance strawberries by up to a month; we can even plant them in grow-bags and get them earlier still in the greenhouse. So you see, growing soft fruits in the garden really is worthwhile and is no more involved than growing anything else.

Strawberries
These are probably the first kind of fruit that a gardener will have a go at growing and, with little attention, good crops can be had the summer after planting. Planting should take place in August or September to be sure of getting a full crop in the first year. Buy them growing in pots for this early planting. Later in the autumn, bare rooted ones are satisfactory but will not carry such a heavy first crop.

The ground should be well prepared and the plants are put in 38 to 45 cm (15 to 18 in) apart with at least 45 cm (18 in) between the rows. If they are going to be cloched, and this should only be done in their first year, the covering is put in place at about the end of February. Apart from keeping the weeds down, the first important job will be to cover the ground beneath the plants with either straw, black polythene or special strawberry mats before the developing fruits touch the ground in June. This will stop them getting splashed with mud and will reduce the risk of slug damage and grey mould (botrytis). Incidentally, spraying against the latter should be carried out every two to three weeks from when the first flowers open until just before picking using a systemic fungicide.

As soon as the crop has been picked, remove the ground covering (straw can go on the compost heap) and cut off all the leaves and old fruit trusses together with any runners that are not wanted for propagation. This gets rid of a lot of pests and diseases and encourages the plants to produce new leaves which help to build up strong fruit buds for the following year. It is time then to feed the plants and the best fertilizer is one that is rich in potash. This encourages fruit bud production and stops growth from being too vigorous. Growmore is as good a material as any but, failing that, a rose or tomato fertilizer is equally suitable and formulated to encourage fruit formation.

Varieties   There are many excellent summer-fruiting varieties:
Cambridge Vigour – one of the earliest; good flavour.
Cambridge Favourite – mainstay of the commercial trade; a regular
heavy cropper, even if its flavour is not first rate.
Redgauntlet – frequently produces a second crop in the autumn,
particularly if the plants were cloched early in the season.
Royal Sovereign – questionably the best flavoured of all, but difficult to
recommend for gardens; light cropper; huge plants susceptible to grey
mould.
Tenira and Maxim – two new varieties with fruits of excellent flavour
without the problem of very large plants; Maxim produces truly huge
fruits.

Autumn-fruiting varieties   The cultivation is much the same as for
maincrop varieties except that planting can take place into the early
spring without reducing the size of the first crop. However, to stop
them fruiting along with the maincrop varieties, the flowers should be
picked off up till the end of May. Obviously strawing is going to be
much later and the plants should not be de-leafed after fruiting. It is
also a good idea to cloche the plants towards the end of September so
that the fruits ripen better and the season is extended for as long as
possible. Ventilation should be given whenever it is warm and sunny
to cut down the incidence of grey mould, which can be a serious
problem that late in the year.

Gento is one of the best varieties though, on the whole, all of them
crop lighter and fruiting is spread over a longer period than the
summer ones. Be sure, also, to plant them in a sunny position; this
helps with the ripening and brings out the best in the flavour.

Raspberries
As a fruit, these are probably just as popular as strawberries but they
do take up a lot more room and need a permanent wire and post
system of support. The posts for this should be no further than 11 m
(36 ft) apart and two wires should be stretched between them 60 cm
(2 ft) and 1.5 m (5 ft) above the ground.

The young canes are planted in the autumn or winter 45 to 60 cm
(1½ to 2 ft) apart, according to the vigour of the variety, and are
immediately cut down to three or four buds high. This encourages new
canes to grow in the following year and prevents a lot of fruit forming
at their expense. The make-up of summer-fruiting raspberries is such
that the canes grow one year and fruit the next so there will be no fruit
the year after planting but plenty thereafter.

These strawberries are having the ground beneath them covered with straw to stop the fruits getting mud splashed. This should be done before the young fruits touch the ground.

After fruiting, the tops of the plants should be cut down to remove any pests and diseases and to encourage strong young foliage to develop.

This illustrates the various things that should be done to strawberries during the summer after they have fruited. The nearest row has been de-leafed and some runners have been pegged down to produce new plants. The next row has been de-leafed and all runners removed. Plants are still fruiting beyond these and both netting and strawberry mats can be clearly seen.

The fruited canes of summer-fruiting raspberries should be cut out as soon as picking is finished along with any weak ones and those growing some distance from the row. The new canes should then be tied in so that they are spaced approximately 10 cm (4 in) apart along the top wire.

During the first summer, weeds should be kept down and it is a good idea to tie the canes to the bottom wire as soon as they are tall enough; tie them to the top wire in the autumn. In the following year, the canes will flower and fruit at the same time as new ones are growing up. After fruiting, the old canes are cut out and the youngsters are tied in for fruiting the following summer. When tying in, aim to space the canes 8 to 10 cm (3 to 4 in) apart; if there are more than are needed, cut the weakest right out. Any canes taller than the top wire should be left for the winter and cut back to 15 to 20 cm (6 to 8 in) above it in the spring. Very tall varieties can have the tops bent over and tied.

Autumn-fruiting raspberries These work on a totally different principle: the canes grow and fruit in the same year. Because they produce new canes prolifically, they are planted 1 m (3 ft) apart and the width of each row needs restricting to no more than 45 cm (18 in) so that a sort of hedge is formed.

No permanent support is needed but a stout stake should still be driven in at each end of the row so that twine can be passed down each side of the canes just before the fruit ripens; this keeps them tidy and stops the fruit getting spoiled. The canes are not cut down after fruiting but are left until the new growth appears in the spring.

Varieties In spite of all the different ones, the earliest variety is ready for picking only ten days before the latest. However, just two of them, Glen Clova and Leo, will give a picking period from very early in July until late August.

Glen Clova – early; vigorous and abundant new canes; good flavour.
Malling Jewel – mid-season; less vigorous; better flavour.
Delight – mid-season; vigorous; large fruits, heavy crops.
Leo – late; vigorous; good flavour; resistant to grey mould.
Zeva (autumn fruiting) – almost certainly the best.

Blackberries

Though not the sort of fruit that everyone would consider growing, they are well worth it if you like them. The cultivated ones may not have quite the flavour of those in the wild but they make up for it in size and cropping. As with raspberries, the canes grow one year and fruit the next, carrying on well into the autumn.

They need post and wire supports. The lowest wire should be 1 m (3 ft) from the ground with either two or three more above it, 30 cm (1 ft) apart. When using the four wire system, the top one is kept for tying the new canes to until after fruiting.

The most common method of training is the 'two way rope' system in which, following removal of the fruited canes in the autumn, the

Opposite: The tayberry is a cross between a blackberry and a raspberry, and has an extremely pleasant flavour

new ones are trained along the three bottom wires on either side of the plant. With a variety like Himalaya, which produces very few new canes, a good practice is to take out the tops of the new canes when they reach the top wire. This encourages the formation of side shoots and avoids the problem of having just one or two canes that may be 4.5 m (15 ft) long. Vigorous varieties like Himalaya and Ashton Cross will need to be planted 3 to 4 m (10 to 13 ft) apart but the weaker Bedford Giant will only need 2.1 to 2.5 m (7 to 8 ft). After planting, the young canes should be cut down to 20 cm (8 in) high.

Varieties

Himalaya – mid-August onwards; very strong grower; heavy cropping.

Bedford Giant – late July onwards; vigorous; weak flavour.

Ashton Cross – early August onwards; very vigorous; good flavour; heavy cropper.

Oregon Thornless – mid-August onwards; medium vigour; good flavour; medium cropper.

Hybrid cane fruits

Most of these are crosses between raspberries and blackberries and, as such, tend to have characteristics from both; the vigour being that of the blackberry and the fruit more like the raspberry. Their support and cultivation is exactly the same as for blackberries.

Loganberries and tayberries should be planted 2.1 to 2.4 m (7 to 8 ft) apart but this should be increased to 3 to 4 m (10 to 13 ft) for sunberries.

Types and varieties

Loganberry (LY 59) – mid-July onwards; moderate vigour; dark red berries.

Thornless loganberry (LY 654) – as above and it crops as heavily.

Tayberry – early July onwards; moderate vigour; fruit like a long raspberry.

Sunberry – mid-July onwards; very strong grower; purplish black fruit.

Gooseberries

These have long been a favourite of gardeners and, even if it is felt that the bushes are a trifle large for a small garden, there is no reason at all why they should not be grown as cordons in the open or against a fence. One of their main virtues is that they can be picked early for cooking or left until they ripen when they are fit for dessert. Probably their worst failing is their thorns and, although work is going on to produce a thornless variety, the nearest we have come is the French variety Captivator, which does still have a few thorns on its branches

Opposite: A well-kept kitchen garden with neat rows of vegetables and a fruit cage to keep the birds at bay

but nowhere near as many as the usual varieties.

When growing gooseberries as bushes, they should be planted 1.5 to 1.8 m (5 to 6 ft) apart and any shoots should be removed from the stem, as well as suckers from amongst the roots to maintain a short 'leg'. They fruit best on the older wood and the aim should be to create a semi-permanent framework of branches carrying short spurs. This also keeps the bushes open and makes picking easier.

The same principles are involved when growing them as cordons except that the young plants are spaced 60 cm (2 ft) apart and are trained to form two upright arms 30 cm (1 ft) apart in the shape of a 'U'. These will need the permanent support of either vertical wires or canes, to which the developing arms are tied. Clearly this is very space-saving and crops are excellent, particularly when grown for dessert as they appreciate the extra sun.

Varieties   There are a great many varieties to choose from but, as most people are mainly concerned with good crops, they can really be reduced to the following:

Careless – the main commercial and cooking variety; medium vigour; heavy crops; mid-season.

Invicta – a new variety that may replace Careless as it crops better; vigorous and thorny.

Leveller – a good dessert variety that crops better than Whitesmith but with slightly less flavour; green/yellow fruits; grown commercially.

Whitesmith – first-rate dessert variety; whitish when ripe; good crops.

Pruning   This should be done as soon as the leaves have fallen in the autumn but, for best results, it should be carried out in conjunction with summer pruning in June which reduces the shade created by all the new shoots.

When a plant is going to be grown as a bush, 10 to 12 branches should be developed and this starts straight after planting when all strong one-year-old shoots are cut back by about half their length. This gives about double the number of shoots in a year's time and probably enough to form the framework of the bush. If it does not, further shortening by half will be required. When there are enough branches, the leading shoots on each one are still shortened by half every winter but any side shoots are cut back to 2 to 3 cm (1 in) or so.

After a few years of cropping, it may be seen that some of the oldest branches are not really pulling their weight; these should be cut right out and new ones built up to replace them.

To form 'U' cordons, retain a couple of good shoots that are growing to the left and right of the main stem and cut out all others. Tie these

The blackberry Himalaya Giant is especially vigorous. Here it can be seen trained to a 1.5-m (5-ft) fence. The tops of the canes were removed in the early summer to induce side shoots to form. This not only produces a more manageable plant but greatly curbs its growth. If the vigour and the thorns still prove too much, it would be better to grow a more civilized variety like Oregon Thornless.

Red currants and gooseberries can easily be grown as 'U' cordons if space is limited. These young plants of Red Lake have already started fruiting. This is what they look like after winter pruning.

With gooseberries, and red currants as well, a more or less permanent framework of branches is built up on which fruiting spurs are encouraged to form.

This is done by cutting back all new shoots to one or two strong buds in the early winter. At the same time, any badly placed, diseased or broken branches are also removed.

two as near horizontally as possible to the wires or canes and cut them back to an upward pointing bud so that the resulting shoot grows up the support. Over the years, the extension growth on each arm is cut back by a third in the autumn. Side shoots are treated as before.

Bushes and cordons both benefit from being pruned in the summer and all this consists of is shortening back the new shoots, except the branch leaders, to five or six leaves once the fruitlets are well developed in June.

Red currants

We will deal with these first because their cultivation is virtually the same as for gooseberries. The only essential difference is that, because they are weaker growers, those to be grown as bushes are planted 1.2 m (4 ft) apart. Cordons are the same at 60 cm (2 ft).

Botanically white currants are just colourless versions of the red currant and so their cultivation is exactly the same.

Varieties

Red Lake – the standard commercial variety; also excellent for gardens.
Jonkheer van Tets – an earlier and heavy cropper; fruit tends to split in a wet season.
Stanza – Where spring frosts are a problem, this one avoids the worst of the trouble by flowering late; red berries, well coloured; moderate flavour.
White Versailles – Generally accepted as the best all-round white currant.

Blackcurrants

These are grown very differently to red currants because they crop best on the young wood so the aim must be to encourage plenty of new shoots to grow from low down each year. These should come not only from near the ground but also from below it. Blackcurrants must never be grown as cordons. Allow 1.2 to 1.8 m (4 to 6 ft) between bushes depending on the quality of the soil.

If this makes it sound as though the bushes will grow too large for a small garden, another method is open to us. Instead of allowing branches to crop for three to four years before cutting them out, as is done traditionally, they are treated more like raspberries in that the individual shoots are allowed to grow for one year and crop in the next. They are then cut out at ground level.

The crop from each bush is less but, by planting them only 60 cm to 1 m (2 to 3 ft) apart, this is more than compensated for and the sideways spread of the bushes is greatly reduced.

Blackcurrants ——————————————— *Growing Fruit*

When planting blackcurrants, make sure that the base of the shoots are 2 to 5 cm (1 to 2 in) below the surface. This is the way to encourage plenty of new shoots so that the bush is kept young and fruitful.

Following planting, blackcurrant bushes must be cut down to within two or three buds of the ground. This may sound harsh treatment but the bush has to be encouraged to establish itself quickly and send up plenty of young shoots the year after planting.

Once the bushes are established and fruiting, the pruning of blackcurrants is more or less confined to removing the older branches that have ceased to be productive along with any that are damaged, diseased, or out of place and those that are causing overcrowding.

Note that the bush now consists almost entirely of strong young shoots. These produce the best quality and quantity of fruit and the aim throughout the life of the bush, which will be 12 to 15 years, must be to maintain a good supply of these every year.

Varieties

Baldwin – main commercial variety for many years; reliable cropper; very susceptible to spring frost damage.

Malling Jet – very late flowering, still carrying fruit in September; excellent where spring frosts are a danger.

Ben Lomond – flowers after but fruits before Baldwin; frequently carries heavier crops.

Tenah – a Dutch variety that crops well; high-quality fruit; ripens over quite a short period.

Pruning   However the bushes are going to be grown, the first job after planting is to cut all shoots down to within two to three buds of the ground. This sounds harsh but it ensures that plenty of new shoots develop in the following year.

When growing the bushes in the traditional way, the only pruning needed for the next two or three years will be the removal of weak shoots and any that are clearly out of place or causing overcrowding. It should not be necessary to remove any tip growth.

Thereafter, two or three of the oldest branches should be cut out each year once they have been cropping for about four years. By that time, they will be getting worn out and will be producing no strong new side shoots.

The bushes must also be kept open so the removal or shortening back of any branches that are in the way should not be neglected. Those that are spreading too far or are too close to the ground should also be cut out.

Protection from birds

Clearly something must be done if we are to protect the fruit from the ravages of thrushes and blackbirds and the only really successful way is to cover the bushes and canes with netting.

There are several makes of fruit cage available today which are relatively cheap and fully effective and this is undoubtedly the tidiest and least troublesome method. However, just as functional are simple lengths of netting draped over the plants when the fruit is starting to show colour. Whichever system is used, do remember that birds can be trapped so regular inspections are needed.

Growing Vegetables

Nowadays it is no longer necessary for every household to have its own vegetable plot; most of what we want can be bought. However, this does have its problems as really fresh vegetables are now only obtainable if we grow our own. Add to this the fact that a single lettuce can cost as much as a packet of seeds that will last the whole summer and the advantages of growing vegetables at home are obvious. Virtually any plot of land can bring forth good crops with the help of modern tools, soil improvers, fertilizers, appropriate varieties and good management.

Planning

The need to plan a garden has already been discussed and nowhere is this more important than when both decorative plants and vegetables are going to be grown.

The one thing that must be avoided at all costs is to relegate vegetables to some out-of-the-way place. Clearly it would be a mistake to give them pride of place but their requirements as regards soil and sunshine are just as great, or even greater than, those of ornamentals. As a general rule, these two sections should be kept apart, both for efficiency and good looks.

It is important to sit down and work out a cropping programme for vegetables. No one can hope to make the most of a vegetable plot if they simply go into a shop in the spring and buy whatever seeds take their fancy. An important consideration is to use the ground to best advantage all the year round. Far too often gardens are only half full during the winter and early spring because the gardener has only planned for the summer and autumn. Making the best use of the land includes intercropping, where quick-maturing or temporary plants are grown between young plants or those that occupy the soil for a long time. Lettuces and radishes are useful in this respect because they can easily be grown between rows of recently planted brassicas.

A phrase that one sometimes comes across is 'successional cropping'. This means making regular sowings of short-lived crops like lettuces or peas so that they mature over a long period. The main

When preparing the ground for sowing all but the largest seeds (such as peas and beans), the plot should be trodden down before the final raking prior to sowing. This will firm the surface, improve the tilth and help the soil to retain moisture.

Use a rake to break down the soil and obtain a fine tilth for a level seed bed ready for sowing.

Here, the gardener is taking out a drill prior to sowing medium-sized seeds, like beetroot; smaller seeds would need a shallower drill. Note that he is using a line; no matter how experienced he is, it is impossible to take out a straight drill without one.

If the soil is dry, it will need watering if seeds are to germinate. To prevent the surface forming a crust above the seeds (capping), the drill should be watered before sowing.

Sowing and thinning —————————————— *Growing Vegetables*

Seeds should be sown thinly along the
length of the drill. After sowing cover the
seeds to their own depth with soil and
tamp firm with the back of the rake.
Always remember to label each row.

Larger seeds such as beans and peas
(shown here) are sown in deeper drills.
Peas are best sown in blocks (see chart on
page 113).

This row of beetroot is being thinned to
one plant every 10 to 13 cm (4 to 5 in).
Thinning should always take place before
the seedlings become overcrowded and the
soil should be gently firmed around those
remaining afterwards. If the weather is
sunny, they should also be watered to
prevent them wilting.

Intercropping is an extremely good way of
making the best use of a limited amount of
land. Take care, though, that neither
crop interferes with the other. Here, the
lettuces will be finished and out of the way
before the dwarf French beans have grown
too big.

These young brassica plants are being lifted from the seed row for planting in their permanent positions. They should be given a good soaking the day before planting out and they must be lifted carefully to preserve as much of the root system as possible.

A dibber is the best tool for planting as it ensures that they are in firmly – especially important for young brassicas. You can test this by holding on to one of the lower leaves and giving it a sharp pull. If the leaf breaks off, planting is firm enough.

Once they are in place, give the plants a good watering. This is made much easier if they are planted in the bottom of a shallow drill, which will also collect water when it rains or when irrigation is applied.

point here, especially for lettuces, is that short rows, or just part of a row, should be sown at one time. This avoids periods of glut. In this way you can usually arrange that as few vegetables as possible come to maturity during your holiday.

Choosing what to grow
The smaller a garden, the more vital it is to decide wisely on what should be grown. This may sound obvious but it is often apparently ignored.

The first consideration is the amount of space needed for a particular crop. Potatoes, for example, take up a lot of room for what they produce; even a single row will occupy a good 1.2 m (4 ft) width of land, which could be used to grow, for example, two rows of peas. On the other hand, even though they take up as much room, a row of runner beans will go on cropping for the best part of four months; certainly one of the most economical vegetables to grow. Personal preference must be taken into account but this must be considered alongside how many of the family like a particular thing. It is pointless to grow something that only one person out of four likes.

Inevitably, economics will come high on the list of considerations. Where only a limited amount of space is available for vegetables, it would be a waste to fill it up with those that can be bought cheaply. Similarly, if a favourite vegetable is hard to buy, then that is the crop one should choose to grow. Winter and early spring is a time of year when vegetables are at their most expensive so anything that can be grown to mature then is going to be a tremendous saving.

Crop rotation
This refers to the practice of not growing similar crops in the same place for two or more years running and it is an important part of the planning operation.

Years ago, very little was known about the needs of individual vegetables and, anyway, more or less the only source of plant foods available was farmyard manure. This provided a good balance of elements but it did not take into account the fact that some crops use more of a given element than others. For example, root crops use a lot of phosphates and potatoes like plenty of potash (see pages 20–21).

Things have changed over the years and today we know all about the likes and dislikes of different vegetables and fertilizers have been developed accordingly. The result of this is that, by using modern fertilizers properly, we can take account of these various foibles and avoid the risk of our soil running short of any particular element.

The main reason for crop rotation is that many vegetables are susceptible to certain individual pests and diseases; for example, brassicas attract club root disease and cabbage root fly, carrots and parsnips are attacked by carrot fly and onions by the white rot fungus. Some of these are carried over in the soil so if susceptible crops are grown where the problem has recently occurred, it is just asking for trouble. (See also pests and diseases chapter.)

Clearly it is not possible in a small garden to stick rigidly to crop rotation but the following table shows what should be aimed for. Group 1 is the most important as all these vegetables are susceptible to club root and, where the disease is known to exist, brassicas should never be followed by brassicas.

THREE-YEAR CROPPING PLAN		
Group 1 **Brassicas**	**Group 2** **Roots**	**Group 3** **Others**
1st year Brussels sprouts Cabbage Cauliflower Kale Savoy Sprouting broccoli Kohl rabi Radish Swede Turnip	Beetroot Carrot Chicory Parsnip Potato	Peas Beans Celery Onions Leeks Lettuce Peppers Spinach Sweet corn Tomatoes Marrows
2nd year Group 3	Group 1	Group 2
3rd year Group 2	Group 3	Group 1

Raising half-hardy vegetables

Half-hardy vegetables are, like flowers, those which will be damaged or killed if the frost catches them. The most common are French and runner beans, sweet corn, tomatoes, peppers, cucumbers, marrows and courgettes. All are safe outdoors once the risk of frost is over some time in May but it does mean that they are best raised under cover and planted out later on. Again as with flowers, they can be sown outside from about mid-May but they will crop much later and, in the case of sweet corn, this may not give the plants enough time to mature at all.

Sowing them under glass during April overcomes the problem and gives them plenty of time to develop and be hardened off before planting them out. If no greenhouse is available, young plants will have to be bought but it is safer to leave this until mid-May unless there is some way of protecting them from frost.

One vegetable throws all these calculations out: potatoes. Their top growth can be frosted after it has emerged from the ground following planting in March or April. This can be guarded against by keeping them regularly earthed up and by being prepared to cover them over with polythene if it looks like being frosty.

Cloches and tunnels

The subject of covering potato tops brings us on to other forms of protection that can be used to help us in the garden. Cloches and tunnels can be bought in all shapes and sizes and may be made from a variety of materials from glass to polythene sheeting.

Their most popular use is to enable crops to be sown earlier in the spring by providing warmer conditions over the seeds. This, though, can be extended so that they are used to cover the ground earlier in the year when it is in a fit state for sowing. By doing this the ground will be kept dry and warm until we are ready to sow a little later on. Cloches are also useful in the autumn for maturing crops like outdoor tomatoes.

Winter protection of vegetables

This can really be divided into two; the protection of standing crops and the storage of vegetables that have been harvested and which are being kept for winter use. In the first section, we are largely concerned with winter brassicas like Brussels sprouts, winter cauliflower and purple-sprouting broccoli – see the illustrations on page 111.

When it comes to storing vegetables, we will be mainly concerned with root crops like carrots, parsnips and potatoes. Although parsnips can be left in the ground until needed, the other two are best lifted and stored. If you have a largely frost-free shed and some straw, they can be kept in bags. You have to watch out for sharp frosts though and this is the point of the straw: use it to cover the bags. Another way is to build a traditional clamp, particularly useful for large quantities. The roots are stacked in heaps and covered over with straw and a layer of earth.

In the spring, earthing-up potatoes is necessary to protect the tops against frost damage.

This polythene tunnel is being used to cover an early sowing of peas. As well as creating a warmer and drier environment, which will lead to quicker germination, the tunnel will also protect the emerged seedlings from the unwelcome attention of sparrows.

Cloches stood up on their ends can be used to protect tomato plants early in the season and to hasten ripening of fruits in the early autumn.

Another use for cloches late in the season. After onions have been lifted they can be laid under cover to dry off thoroughly before storing. Make sure the ends of the cloches are left open so there is free circulation of air.

Winter cauliflowers can be protected from the worst of the frost either by bending a leaf over the curd or by pulling off one of the lower leaves and placing it over the centre.

Winter brassicas, in particular Brussels sprouts, benefit from being staked in winter. This prevents the plants from being rocked or blown over by the wind and keeps them firmly rooted.

An outdoor 'clamp' is perfectly safe for storing parsnips or carrots through the winter but potatoes are better kept in sacks in a shed or outhouse to ensure the frost doesn't get at them. Cover them first with straw and then a layer of earth to keep them nice and cosy.

A selection of vegetables

This does not profess to be a complete list of vegetables but it does give an idea of those that can be grown in any garden. Varietal names are not given because new ones are introduced every year and any list would be out of date once new seed catalogues are issued. Where the spacing is given, the first figure refers to the distance between the plants and the second to that between the rows. Some of them may vary from those given in catalogues and on seed packets but they are based on the very latest available from the National Vegetable Research Station, Wellesbourne, England, and are aimed at producing maximum yields rather than show-quality vegetables.

TABLE OF SELECTED VEGETABLES					
Crop	Sowing time	Planting time	Spacing	Natural season	Storage
Beetroot	from Apr. to June		thin to 10 × 18 cm (4 × 7 in)	June to winter	pickle or clamp
Beans *(broad)*	Nov. or from Feb. to Apr.		12 × 45 cm (4½ × 18 in)	summer	freeze
Beans *(runner)*	outdoors in May		15 × 60 cm (6 × 24 in)	late summer to autumn	freeze or salt
Beans *(dwarf French)*	late Apr. to June		5 × 45 cm (2 × 18 in)	summer	freeze
Broccoli *(sprouting)*	Mar. to May	Apr. to June	60 × 60 cm (24 × 24 in)	Mar./Apr.	freeze
Brussels sprouts	Mar. to Apr.	May to June	1 × 1 m (36 × 36 in)	autumn and winter	freeze
Cabbage *(spring)*	Aug.	Sept. to Oct.	10 × 30 cm (4 × 12 in) use later to end up at 30 × 30 cm (12 × 12 in)	May/June	
Cabbage *(summer)*	Mar. and Apr.	Apr. and May	45 × 45 cm (18 × 18 in)	July/Aug.	
Cabbage *(winter)*	Apr. and May	May and June	45 × 45 cm (18 × 18 in)	Oct. to Apr.	
Carrots	Mar. to July		7 × 15 cm (2½ × 6 in)	summer to winter	freeze or clamp
Cauliflower *(summer)*	Mar. to May	Apr. to June	50 × 50 cm (20 × 20 in)	July/Aug.	freeze
Cauliflower *(autumn)*	May	June	70 × 70 cm (28 × 28 in)	Sept. to Dec.	freeze

Crop	Sowing time	Planting time	Spacing	Natural season	Storage
Cauliflower (*winter*)	Apr. and May	May and June	thin to 75 × 75 cm (30 × 30 in)	Feb. to Apr.	
Leeks	Mar. and Apr.	June	15 × 30 cm (6 × 12 in)	autumn and winter	freeze
Lettuce	Mar. to July		23 × 23 cm (9 × 9 in)	June to Nov.	
Marrows and courgettes	May		75 cm (30 in)	summer and autumn	hang up marrows
Onions	Mar. (Japanese varieties in autumn)	plant sets in Mar. or autumn	thin to 10 × 25 cm (4 × 10 in) plant sets 10 × 25 cm (4 × 12 in)	Aug. to spring	hang up in net bags
Parsnips	Feb. to Apr.		thin to 10 × 23 cm (4 × 9 in)	autumn and winter	clamps
Peas	Mar. to June		10 × 10 cm (4 × 4 in) in blocks of 3 rows 45 cm (18 in) between blocks	June to Sept.	freeze
Potatoes (*earlies*)		mid- to late Mar.	30–40×75 cm (12–16×30 in)	late May to Aug.	
Potatoes (*maincrop*)		late Apr. to early May	40 × 75 cm (16 × 30 in)	Sept. to Apr. if stored well	in bags
Radish	Mar. to Aug.		sow thinly	summer to winter	
Ridge cucumber	late May		1 m (36 in)	summer and autumn	
Sweet corn	May		40 × 40 cm (16 × 16 in) 2 seeds per station	Aug./Sept.	freeze
Tomatoes	May		50 × 50 cm (20 × 20 in)	Aug. to Dec.	
Turnips	late Mar. to July		thin to 8 × 38 cm (3 × 15 in)	May to winter	clamps

Pests, Diseases and Weed Control

To many people, pest and disease control begins and ends with a sprayer full of chemical. Certainly this has a useful part to play because there is bound to come a time when chemicals are the only sensible solution. At the other end of the scale, a large number of gardeners object to the use of chemicals just because they are chemicals.

The answer lies somewhere between these two rather short-sighted approaches. Everything should be done to deter pests and diseases but, in the final analysis, chemicals may well be the only practical answer.

Cultural control
This refers to what we as gardeners can do to delay and lessen attacks by both pests and diseases. The first thing is to grow plants well. Those that are strong and robust are far less likely to succumb to minor attacks and, in fact, it is almost certain that a strongly growing plant has some built-in resistance.

Next, we must always guard against creating conditions that are likely to be conducive to pests and diseases. This is more applicable to the greenhouse, where we have a greater control over the environment, but it can also be practised outdoors. For example, seedlings are much more susceptible to fungus diseases when they are cramped together and clearly overcrowded. Similarly, in the greenhouse, it is well known that hot and dry conditions are much appreciated by the red spider mite.

Hygiene in the garden and the greenhouse are also important. This does not mean pouring disinfectant all over everything but it does mean that all plant debris, such as old vegetable leaves, should be cleared up regularly and often. Not only does rubbish attract our old enemy grey mould (botrytis) but it also provides perfect housing conditions for things like slugs and snails.

Weeds must be attended to as well. Apart from the competition they represent to our cultivated plants, they can catch and spread diseases and pests in just the same way as any other plant.

For instance, club root of brassicas will also attack the weed shepherd's purse, as well as the different cresses, all members of the same family. The importance of this comes home when taken in conjunction with crop rotation. This is going to be a pointless exercise if weeds are allowed to remain to carry the disease over from season to season. Crop rotation itself is a very important part of good gardening.

Plant breeders are spending a lot of time on developing varieties that are resistant to specific diseases and we should always take advantage of these when we see them in the seed catalogues.

Chemical control
In spite of all these precautions, the time will surely come when we have to enlist the help of chemicals and, to get the best results, we should follow a definite sequence.

This starts with early and correct identification of the problem. Every gardener should be on the look-out for trouble the whole time so that, when it arises, action can be taken quickly. The problem is thus contained before it has time to spread, the plants suffer less damage and a much smaller quantity of chemical is needed.

Even in these days of near 'cure-all' chemicals, it is still important to find out what the trouble is. Damage done to plants by several different pests can look very similar to the untrained eye but the same chemical is not necessarily effective against all of them. If you have trouble in identifying something, seek advice from other gardeners or horticultural societies and, once it has a name, find the correct chemical to treat it. At the same time, it must be determined whether or not the chosen remedy is safe to use on the plants in question. This will be found on the label along with any safety interval that has to elapse between treating vegetables or fruits and eating them.

Chemicals are available as sprays, dusts, aerosols and smokes. For outdoor work, sprays are best as they give good coverage of the plant. However, if an outbreak is small or only a few plants need treating, an aerosol is handier as it does away with the need to mix up relatively large amounts of spray, much of which will then have to be disposed of safely.

Dusts leave unsightly deposits on plants so are really best kept for treating the ground against soil-borne pests and diseases and things like ants.

In a greenhouse, smokes and aerosols are the most effective because of their fumigant action.

Amongst the bewildering array of bottles and packets, some will be seen to be labelled 'systemic'. These materials are actually absorbed by the plant's leaves and are passed around in the sap stream to a greater or lesser extent to other parts of the plant.

Clearly, this will protect the plants more effectively and the chemical cannot be washed off by rain once it has been absorbed.

Biological pest control

In recent years, a method of controlling pests in greenhouses that does not involve chemicals has gained in popularity. This is by introducing the natural enemies of pests.

Two such creatures are available to gardeners, one to control white fly and the other red spider mite. If they are introduced when the pests are first seen, numbers will be kept down to a harmless level for the rest of the season. However, these predators are only available by mail order, so keep your eyes open for advertisements in the gardening press early in the summer.

Weeds

The first thing that occurs to gardeners when weeds are mentioned is that they should be got rid of because they make the place untidy. This is certainly a very important aspect but there are other more damaging ones as well.

The part they play in harbouring pests and diseases has been touched on but their worst crime is that of competing with cultivated plants for water and food as well as space above and below ground. This does not have serious implications for established plants if the weeds are small but, turn the situation round and allow weeds to dominate a row of seedlings and the results can be disastrous.

Control   The hoe has always been the traditional tool for killing weeds and, once bought, it costs nothing but energy to use whereas chemicals can be expensive.

There are though certain places and occasions when a weedkiller is far more effective or, indeed, the only thing that is likely to be successful. Paths and drives are an obvious place for weedkillers. Even if the weeds are killed by some other means, there is nothing to stop fresh ones emerging, but the use of a weedkiller based on simazine (many brands available) will keep away weeds for a year or more.

Weeds amongst roses and shrubs are also difficult to control but, once they have been cleared with a paraquat and diquat formulation like 'Weedol', an application of Covershield which contains prop-achlor can prevent any more appearing for up to six months. Even problem weeds like couch grass and bindweed are quite easy to kill with any one of several products so if a position is reached where there seems to be no other solution, Tumbleweed, containing glyphosate, can be used against both couch and bindweed. Weed Out, containing alloxydim-sodium, should be used against couch growing among broad-leaved plants.

Using chemicals
Although many garden chemicals are potentially dangerous, they are perfectly safe if used with common sense and if the manufacturer's instructions on the container are followed to the letter. This applies equally well to household chemicals like bleach and ammonia so those we use in the garden are certainly not in a class of their own.

The product labels are so packed with instructions for their safe and effective use that it is unnecessary to cover the same ground here but there is one piece of advice that cannot be repeated too often:
READ AND UNDERSTAND ALL LABELS BEFORE USING ANY CHEMICAL
One point that often worries gardeners is the safe disposal of chemicals. If it is merely some that is left over in the sprayer, the best solution is to offer it to a neighbour. Failing that, it is perfectly safe to tip it down the lavatory or an outside drain; the amount of water that it will come into contact with will dilute it beyond all recognition. The same goes for liquid concentrates that have lost their labels. Dry materials should be put in the dustbin.

The safety of the actual user is often ignored by gardeners. The most rudimentary precaution is always to wear rubber gloves when handling garden chemicals of any sort, damaging or not. Spraying should never be carried out when it is windy for fear of the spray being blown to where it can cause harm; nor should it be done in bright sunshine because even plain water can magnify the sun's rays enough to scorch plants.

Control of the more common pests and diseases
In most cases, pests and diseases should be acted against as soon as they appear and it is really only necessary with fruit trees and bushes to take steps in advance of an outbreak. The other exceptions to this policy are with the control of mildew and black spot of roses. These fungus diseases are more or less bound to occur every year and regular spraying is going to be needed from just after growth starts in the spring.

Here are a couple of charts to help you; the first is a general one giving the control measures needed against various problems. The other is concerned with fruit crops alone.

As most chemicals are sold under a variety of brand names, only the

chemical name is given but any good shop or garden centre will be able
to supply an appropriate brand.

PESTS	CHEMICAL
Ants	*borax, chlordane, pyrethrum*
Aphids (greenfly)	*dimethoate, permethrin, pirimicarb*
Cabbage root fly	*bromophos, diazinon, phoxim*
Capsid bug	*dimethoate, fenitrothion*
Carrot fly	*as for cabbage root fly*
Caterpillars	*gamma-*HCH, *permethrin, trichlorphon*
Cutworms	*as for cabbage root fly*
Earwigs	*gamma-*HCH
Cuckoo spit (leafhoppers)	*dimethoate, fenitrothion*
Leafminers	*malathion*
Leatherjackets	*as for cabbage root fly*
Millepedes	*as for cabbage root fly*
Onion fly	*as for cabbage root fly*
Red spider mite	*dimethoate*
Slugs and snails	*metaldehyde, methiocarb*
Whitefly	*permethrin, malathion*
Wireworm	*as for cabbage root fly, gamma-*HCH

DISEASES	
Black spot (roses)	*benomyl, carbendazim, thiophanate-methyl*
Blight (potatoes)	*copper, mancozeb*
Botrytis (grey mould)	*as for black spot*
Club root (of brassicas)	*calomel, thiophanate-methyl*
Damping off (of seedlings)	*copper*
Mildew (roses etc.)	*as for black spot*
Rust (roses, mint etc.)	*mancozeb, propiconazole*
Storage diseases	*benomyl, sulphur, thiophanate-methyl*

Pests and diseases of fruit Fruit crops, particularly apples, are best
treated routinely each year. Otherwise it is often too late to effect a
treatment by the time the outbreak has been noticed. The following
chart lists the main problems that need regular control. Although the
chemicals recommended are not the only ones suitable for the
particular job, they are the ones generally considered to be the most
effective and are widely available.

Crop	Pest or disease	When to spray	Chemical
Tree and bush fruit	overwintering insects and eggs	winter, after leaf-fall	tar oil winter wash
Apples and pears	apple and pear scab	fortnightly once leaves are open	benomyl, thiophanate-methyl
Apples and pears	mildew	fortnightly once leaves are open	benomyl, thiophanate-methyl
Pears	pear midge	just before flowers open	fenitrothion
Apples	apple sawfly	after petal-fall	fenitrothion, HCH
Apples	codling moth	early and mid-June	permethrin
Apples and pears	storage rots	dip fruits after picking	benomyl, thiophanate-methyl
Peaches	peach leaf curl	after leaf-fall and when leaves are open in spring	copper
Soft fruit	botrytis (grey mould)	fortnightly after blossom has fallen	benomyl, thiophanate-methyl
Raspberries	raspberry beetle	when first fruit is pink	fenitrothion
Gooseberries	gooseberry sawfly	soon after fruit sets	dimethoate

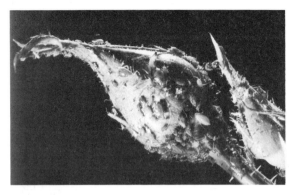

We tend to lump all aphids together and call them 'greenfly', although there are, in fact, several different kinds. Besides causing a general weakening of the host plant by sucking the sap, many species of aphids are responsible for spreading plant virus diseases. Aphids can all be controlled with a systemic insecticide or, if there are beneficial insects present which you do not wish to kill (ladybirds or bees), use Rapid or Abol G.

This kind of leaf damage is not easy to identify. It is caused by the aptly named leafhopper; not a serious pest but quite common. It can carry virus disease particularly to strawberries, so a systemic insecticide used for aphid control should be used. In spring the cuckoo spit secreted by young leafhoppers is a familiar sight.

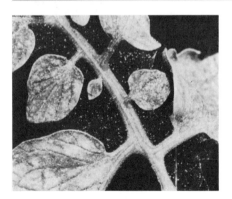

Red spider mite can be a serious pest in the greenhouse or outdoors in a dry summer. The mites are barely visible but cause leaves to become speckled yellow and, in bad cases, bring growth to a complete halt. Spray with a systemic insecticide based on dimethoate early, before the pests build up.

Besides preventing the infested buds (left) from opening, big-bud mite or blackcurrant gall mite is responsible for spreading the virus disease, reversion. The only sure control is to remove and burn the swollen buds in the winter or, if there are many, to destroy the whole bush, as it will almost certainly have reversion disease.

Leafminer caterpillars tunnel in foliage and can completely ruin chrysanthemums and many other plants. The damage is done by the little grubs tunnelling into the leaf under the outer 'skin'. Control measures are needed before they start burrowing. Under glass, an HCH smoke gives good control whilst outside a spray of gamma-HCH or malathion will be needed.

The caterpillar illustrated is that of the large white butterfly which attacks brassicas. The caterpillar problem is at its worst from July onwards. Where there are just a few, they can be picked off but with a severe outbreak Bio Long-Last, a caterpillar and whitefly killer, derris or fenitrothion will be effective.

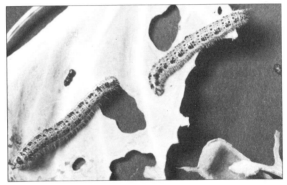

The carrot fly grub also attacks parsnips. It tunnels into the roots and provides points of entry for a number of soil-borne diseases as well. A similar pest attacks onions. Both pests can be controlled by treating the soil surface around the young plants gamma-HCH dust (Lindane) or an appropriate soil insecticide.

Cabbage root fly attacks all types of brassicas. The damage to the root system can be severe. The pest can be controlled by a granular soil insecticide or by these specially designed collars. Put one around each plant after transplanting to provide a very effective non-chemical way of preventing cabbage root fly damage.

The blistered and reddened leaves of peach leaf curl start appearing in the early spring and nearly always drop prematurely so that the tree is progressively weakened. A copper fungicide should be applied during leaf-fall and again shortly after growth has started in spring.

Apple canker can seriously affect certain varieties, e.g. Cox, growing in poorly drained ground. The fungus enters through a wound and spreads outwards until, frequently, the shoot or branch is girdled and dies. Cut away the dead and brown bark into healthy wood and treat with a fungicidal paint.

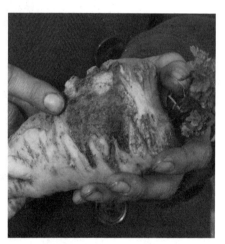 

Parsnip canker is in no way connected to apple canker; it is a fungus that lives in the soil and gains entry through wounds, such as those made by hoeing or the carrot fly. It affects broad-shouldered, stump-rooted varieties worst of all. Avoiding the causes is really the only control.

Club root disease can be crippling amongst all members of the brassica family, including weeds like shepherd's purse. Crop rotation can help but the most effective control is to prevent the soil getting too acidic by applying lime and using a club root dip before planting.

Diseases and disorders

A disorder of tomatoes brought on by erratic watering is blossom end rot. This is not a disease but a physiological problem connected with a lack of calcium. However, keeping the soil or compost evenly moist is the best prevention.

'Balling' is a problem sometimes encountered with the more multi-petalled rose varieties. The outer petals go brown and the flowers fail to develop. It is normally associated with wet weather and is frequently accompanied by botrytis. Regular spraying against black spot and mildew will usually keep the problem under control.

A most serious rose disease is mildew, a white powdery covering of the new shoots and leaves which is easily visible. Though some varieties are more susceptible than others, not one is completely immune. Pruning can alleviate the problem by increasing the circulation of air around the plant. Affected shoots should be removed and then burnt. Regular spraying with a rose fungicide will keep the problem under control.

Black spot is another serious disease of roses. Again, some varieties are more susceptible than others and complete control is virtually impossible. Regular spraying with a rose fungicide throughout the growing season will go a long way towards keeping on top of the problem, together with collecting and burning affected leaves.

Weed control

Hoeing is an effective method of weed control providing that it is done while they are still young. In dry, sunny weather the weeds will wilt and die but if the soil is wet they can take root again unless cleared up. This onion hoe is a handy tool to use in small borders and around vegetables.

Hedge bottoms are notorious weed traps which can lead to weeds flowering and seeding themselves in other parts of the garden. If you rely on controlling them by hand, be sure to take action before they have run to seed, as they have in this case.

A residual weedkiller applied in the spring is an effective method of killing seedling weeds and will keep the area weed-free for up to a year. Weedex, based on simazine, is one of the best formulations but check that it is safe to use by your particular plants.

Although the indiscriminate use of garden chemicals is to be frowned upon, there are occasions when they are invaluable, i.e. when clearing waste land, steps and paths. The near section of this path has been treated with a path weedkiller based on simazine (a number of brands are widely available). If this is applied in early spring it will keep the path or area of land clear of weeds well into the following winter.

Month by Month in the Garden

January

Lawns Prepare for spring sowing; brush off dead leaves; overhaul machinery.

Vegetables Continue digging when weather permits; prepare cropping programme; order seeds.

Fruit Carry on pruning and planting when conditions are suitable; apply tar oil winter wash to fruit trees and bushes.

Flowers & Shrubs Remove snow from trees and shrubs; inspect dahlia tubers and gladioli corms in store.

February

Lawns Give grass a high cut if needed; continue turfing and preparing for sowing.

Vegetables Finish digging; make an early sowing of broad beans.

Fruit Continue pruning and planting when conditions are suitable; spray peaches against peach leaf curl.

Flowers & Shrubs Continue planting; apply simazine weedkiller to paths and drives.

March

Lawns Apply mosskiller/fertilizer formulation or fertilizer alone; start regular mowing if needed and weather permitting; rake to remove debris and spike to aerate.

Vegetables Sow Brussels sprouts, summer cabbage, celery, lettuces, leeks, peas, onions, parsnips and radishes when conditions are suitable.

Fruit Finish pruning and planting.

Flowers & Shrubs Plant evergreens and finish planting others; prune and feed roses.

April

Lawns Sow new lawns; continue turfing; start regular mowing; reduce height of cut by adjusting blade on mower.

Vegetables Sow beetroots, turnips, carrots, cauliflowers and autumn cabbage in the open; French and runner beans and sweet corn under cloches and outdoor tomatoes and cucumbers in the greenhouse; plant potatoes.

Fruit Start spraying against pests and diseases except during blossom time.

Flowers & Shrubs Finish planting evergreens and conifers; sow hardy annuals; thin out seedlings; apply a mulch as required.

May

Lawns Continue feeding; water new lawns if needed; start weed control.

Vegetables Sow half-hardies in open; thin seedlings; plant out brassicas.

Fruit Spray as necessary; spread straw beneath strawberries.

Flowers & Shrubs Replace spring bedding plants at end of month; plant dahlias and other half-hardies; sow biennials, including wallflowers.

June
Lawns   Continue weed control; rake to lift seed heads.
Vegetables   Sow swedes and continue successional sowings; carry out
                   pest and disease control.
Fruit   Straw down strawberries; summer prune gooseberries and
                   red currants.
Flowers   Finish planting half-hardies; prune shrubs that have flowered.
& Shrubs

July
Lawns   Raise height of cut on mower and water during drought; prepare for
                   autumn sowing.
Vegetables   Continue sowing lettuces and radishes; water as necessary.
Fruit   Remove straw from fruited strawberries and propagate runners.
Flowers   Remove flower heads as they fade; tie in new growth on climbers.
& Shrubs

August
Lawns   Sow towards end of month; continue weed control and feeding.
Vegetables   Sow spring cabbages; plant out winter and spring brassicas.
Fruit   Prune raspberries after fruiting; summer prune trained fruit trees.
Flowers   Continue dead-heading; take semi-ripe cuttings of shrubs.
& Shrubs

September
Lawns   Finish sowing; finish weed control; apply last summer fertilizer.
Vegetables   Sow lettuces for the spring; prepare onions for harvest.
Fruit   Finish planting strawberries; pick plums, apples and pears.
Flowers   Plant conifers and evergreens and spring flowering bulbs.
& Shrubs

October
Lawns   Rake, spike and top-dress; repair broken edges; start turfing.
Vegetables   Lift root vegetables for storage; earth up celery and leeks.
Fruit   Finish picking apples and pears for storage.
Flowers   Finish planting evergreens, conifers and bulbs; replace or clear
& Shrubs   summer bedding plants; lift gladioli, dahlias and other half-hardy
                   flowering plants; take hardwood cuttings.

November
Lawns   Finish regular mowing and autumn maintenance; continue turfing.
Vegetables   Protect cauliflowers from frost; start digging when conditions are
                   suitable.
Fruit   Start planting and pruning; take currant and gooseberry cuttings.
Flowers   Cut back roses; finish planting spring bedding; lift, divide and plant
& Shrubs   herbaceous perennials.

December
Lawns   Continue turfing; remove dead leaves; get mower serviced and
                   attend to other machinery.
Vegetables   Continue digging; examine stored vegetables for any sign of disease.
Fruit   Continue pruning and planting when conditions are suitable; start
                   applying tar-oil winter wash to fruit trees and bushes.
Flowers   Protect semi-hardy plants from severe weather by covering them with
& Shrubs   bracken; clear up borders.

Index